I0163282

WAVES OF
GRACE & GLORY

WAVES OF
GRACE & GLORY

90 Uplifting Articles

SUSAN ROSE

ABUNDANCE
PRESS

Book Contents and Cover Images © 2016 by Susan Rose

Published by Abundance Press, United States of America.

All rights reserved. This book or any portion thereof may not be reproduced or used in any manner whatsoever without the express written permission of the author, except for the use of brief quotations in a book review.

Author may be contacted through her website: intothedeep.net.

Cover scene photographed at Ano Nuevo State Park, California, USA.

Unless otherwise noted, scripture quoted herein is New King James Version.

Alternate scripture versions quoted herein are AMPC (Amplified Classic), ESV (English Standard Version), NASB (New American Standard Bible), NIV (New International Version) and NLT (New Living Translation).

ISBN-13: 978-0692790687
ISBN-10: 0692790683

Dedicated to the Ones I Love

May you rise each day with the glory of God upon you—always being filled with His Spirit—always seeing, hearing, knowing, and speaking the beautiful truth of the Lord.

Contents

Introduction

The title of this book, "Waves of Grace & Glory," has a twofold purpose. Primarily, it refers to what God is sending forth on a large scale. Christian prayer has opened gates, and God is releasing powerful waves of grace and glory to flood the scene.

Prayer from believers of today is merging perfectly with prayer from past generations—from Christians who prayed long ago for the future of the Church. The Spirit of God has inspired and choreographed this past-and-present prayer, putting strong focus on the "last days" we're living in now. This collective storm of intercession is a unified plea for help regarding "such a time as this." *Now, a vast archive of prayer awaits the timing of God.* I believe the season is upon us for His response to be unleashed. (See Isaiah 60.) I look for it to come in large waves. *Why?* Because the Lord has given me dreams and visions of gigantic waves for several years, and the context has always been one of tremendous, overwhelming blessing.

The book title also refers to the content: a collection of 90 inspired articles that come as waves, one right after another. If you're willing, they will crash right over you—washing, encouraging, and reviving you with life-giving truth.

God has an important plan for each of our lives. You'll find this theme sprinkled liberally throughout my writing. It is particularly valuable to me because my own modest life gained new energy when I learned that I'm destined for significance. I believe this precept should be clearly and loudly announced.

God wants to communicate on a personal level with *all* Christians, not just the prophetically gifted. I passionately promote the necessity of hearing the voice of God, in whatever ways He chooses to speak. Anyone can read the Bible, but only the Spirit of God can breathe life into it, consequently speaking through its text—and we must hear this Voice. Through personal experience, I know the Spirit also sends discernment into our thoughts and our dreams. He gives us revelation through various types of visions, and He often speaks through nature.

Interaction with the Lord is exciting! The longest chapter, "Encountering God Each Day," is devoted to this topic, giving many personal examples. I hope to entice readers into the reality of God as I know Him—and further, if they dare.

My writing began in earnest around 2000, when God told me through a prophet to *"Write. Just keep writing."* This confirmed His personal words to me about not wasting the "talent" that He's given me (Matthew 25:14-30). I have thoroughly enjoyed my assignment to write. God has been close by my side, helping me compose these varied and unique edifications from His heart. Now, sixteen years later, I have written more than 350 inspirational articles. I've divided them into categories, five of which are included in this collection.

Please keep the following in mind as you read my book:

- My strong desire is to encourage and enlighten the Christians who have grown tired of lifeless, pharisaic teaching, and with theology that puts God in a small, quiet, predictable box. I write to those who hunger for more.

- Each article stands alone, so readers can skip around. It was never my intention to write a series of teachings on one theme. I simply wrote what God put on my heart, and He often repeated Himself. So, when you notice a trend, please embrace the emphasis. And when you find a variety of perspectives, please receive them as multiple facets of larger truth.

- I've included the dates of writing to give readers perspective regarding seasons and events. The articles are not in chronological order, but instead are grouped by subject. You'll find that generally, the newer articles are a little longer, but the shorter ones are no less important.

Where space allows, my articles are followed by lined areas for making notes. Please take time to meditate and listen for the Spirit to tailor the message to fit you personally, then write down what He says. God is always pleased when we put value on His words.

I pray that you will be uplifted and filled with hope by the words in this book. May you always have eyes that see and ears that hear (Matthew 13:16), along with a heart that beats in tune with the heart of God.

I join you in great expectation of the Lord,

Susan Rose

For the Lord of hosts has purposed, and who will annul it?
His hand is stretched out, and who will turn it back?

Isaiah 14:27

GRACE & GLORY

Grace Abounds

August 8, 2008

Moreover the law entered that the offense might abound. But where sin abounded, grace abounded much more... - Romans 5:20.

When making his point to the Romans, Paul wrote these words in past tense. But they are just as true today. We still have plenty of sin in this world, so grace continues to abound "much more."

Because God "makes His sun rise on the evil and on the good, and sends rain on the just and on the unjust" (Matthew 5:45), a certain amount of grace is given to all who live and breathe. But to enter the overwhelming flood of God's generosity, Christians must use the key of faith. If the crumbs that fall to the unsaved world no longer satisfy you, then rise up and boldly claim the banquet that is yours.

Therefore, having been justified by faith, we have peace with God through our Lord Jesus Christ, through whom also we have access by faith into this grace in which we stand, and rejoice in hope of the glory of God - Romans 5:1-2.

Open your Bible, and let God's word light up your heart and your life. Learn that His grace, flowing through you, will make a positive impact in this broken, needy world.

Dear Lord, we thank You for the tidal wave of glory and grace that is ready to crash over us in these last days. Please make us ready for all that it brings. Revive our faith and fire up our expectations.

_____

_____

_____

_____

_____

Targeted by Glory

January 27, 2014

Consider it all joy, my brethren, when you encounter various trials, knowing that the testing of your faith produces endurance. And let endurance have its perfect result, so that you may be perfect and complete, lacking in nothing. But if any of you lacks wisdom, let him ask of God, who gives to all generously and without reproach, and it will be given to him - James 1:2-5 NASB.

Much to the enemy's dismay, our "various trials" provide targets for the glory of God. Life-changing truth and exceptional blessing are always available to us, but they need a suitable place of application. That's where our trials come into play. Maybe God wants to make us more humble, but we're totally unaware of our need for this change. Or maybe He wants to increase our patience, but we don't have a clue about our deficit. Then along come stressful conditions that reveal our weakness in these areas. Our exposure is painful and humiliating, but it's also very enlightening. With our eyes now open, we can agree with God about our sin, and He will help us submit to His methods for change. *Thus, God's glory hits its target.*

Our view of God's kingdom will always be enlarged when we are tested. These challenges are choreographed to help us observe personal sin that might go unnoticed in a more peaceful setting. After we've adjusted our behavior according to God's direction, then (and *only* then) we can look at the sources and patterns of sin in the lives of those who disturb us. At this point, we're able to effectively pray and set them free from enemy strongholds.

You shall also be a crown of glory in the hand of the Lord, and a royal diadem in the hand of your God – Isaiah 62:3.

For the struggling Christian whose heart is set on pleasing the Lord, it's empowering to know that His glory invades our lives to help. Our entire being has become His target. But even with God's glory resting heavily upon us, we don't want to camp a minute longer than is necessary in the hard places of testing. Being made in God's image, we always yearn for peace. So, just as Jacob did at Peniel, I suggest that we wrestle with God during our days of trouble and refuse to let Him go until we are blessed

(Genesis 32:22-32). As we wrestle by way of prayer, we can be certain that God is pleased. We can be sure that He will answer.

As we wait for Your perfect response to our prayers, dear Lord, we rest and bask in the light of Your love. You have promised healing, provision, and promotion. You have promised a "broad place" for us to reign with righteousness and purpose. Let Your blessings arrive soon so we can increase our help to others. We thank You, Lord, for sharing Your vision so we can join in Your plans. Thank You for aiming Your glory directly at us.

_____

_____

_____

_____

_____

_____

_____

_____

_____

_____

_____

_____

_____

God Always Keeps His Word

September 19, 2018

"You only have a problem if I cannot be trusted." That was the message God impressed upon me as I woke from an afternoon nap. I'm sharing this today to encourage those of you who may be afraid.

For each of us, the needs of life (apart from needing God) can be divided into three major categories—health, finances, and relationships. There are certainly subcategories, but I believe they all fit under the three main umbrellas.

We usually get to deal with one, two, or all three of these "major categories" during any given season. I have been blessed with the challenge of dealing with all three areas at the current time. My health issues are all minor, except for one that will require surgery if God doesn't intervene. My finances can be described as "right on the edge." My family relationships have been under heavy enemy fire, and damage has been sustained.

The good news for me is that God has given me glorious personal promises in each of these areas.

IF YOU DON'T HAVE PERSONAL PROMISES FROM THE LORD, PLEASE DRAW NEAR TO HIM UNTIL YOU RECEIVE THESE TREASURES FROM HIS HEART.

Before I even knew about a particular health matter, God graciously gave me a vision of me being healed from head to toe. The vision focused on the most worrisome issue, so when it arose about a year later, I had that beautiful promise to fall back on. Whenever the enemy pokes me with his "stick of fear," I can lean on God's word to me. The issue with finances is exactly the same. On April 5, 2008, the Lord revealed His plan to me for "prosperity." (That was a glorious day!) This plan is beyond exciting, and God has confirmed it many times. Now, when my little boat begins to rock, I remember the promise of great provision, and I REST in it. Regarding my family, the Lord has assured me repeatedly, in numerous ways, that my dearest ones will be saved and that love will be restored.

God said, "You ONLY have a problem if I cannot be trusted." Well I know He CAN be trusted because He is completely and perfectly faithful. Having lifetime experience with God's character is helpful, but His Word is even better:

He will cover you with his feathers; you will take refuge under his wings. His faithfulness will be a protective shield – Psalm 91:4.

Let us hold fast the confession of our hope without wavering, for He who promised is faithful - Hebrews 10:23.

God is not man, that he should lie, or a son of man, that he should change his mind. Has he said, and will he not do it? Or has he spoken, and will he not fulfill it? - Numbers 23:19.

Dear Lord, I'm so very thankful for the personal promises you've given me over the years. Combined with Your Word, these promises have lifted me high above the storms of life. My fears have been calmed, and my wounds have been healed. Lord, please help us all to hear and see and know what is in Your heart for us. Thank You, Lord, for Your glorious grace.

_____

_____

_____

_____

_____

_____

_____

_____

His Glory is Upon Us

November 25, 2014

Are you going through a difficult time that is severely testing your faith? Are you anxious about the condition of your family, your finances, your health, or the chaotic world around you? Are you often focused on negative details, letting them take the reins of your mind for much too long? If your answers are "Yes," then I know you are wanting change. But to see it arrive, you must direct your thoughts to what God says about your troubles and to the part He wants you to play in His solution.

...let us lay aside every weight, and the sin which so easily ensnares us, and let us run with endurance the race that is set before us, looking unto Jesus, the author and finisher of our faith, who for the joy that was set before Him endured the cross, despising the shame, and has sat down at the right hand of the throne of God – Hebrews 12:1-2.

"Let us lay aside every weight" means that we must give up any activity that weighs us down by draining our time and energy. No matter how virtuous the activity, if it's not in God's plan for our day, then we should set it down and walk away.

Also, we must "lay aside...the sin which so easily ensnares us." To be in a position of spiritual power, we cannot play around with sin. Even "little sins" will keep us on a path of mediocrity that leads to nowhere good.

We must run the race before us with endurance, "looking unto Jesus" as our example and our strength. When we're given a difficult task or a challenging situation, then we must embrace it just like Jesus embraced the cross because of the glory that lies beyond it.

But maybe your trial has lasted for years. Your faith has grown, but so has the intensity of demonic attacks. Your heart is heavy, and you struggle to worship God—just what the enemy had in mind. If this describes your personal situation, then get ready to be encouraged! God has a word for you today:

Arise, shine; for your light has come! And the glory of the Lord is risen upon you. For behold, the darkness shall cover the earth, and deep darkness the people; but the Lord will arise over you, and His glory will be seen upon you – Isaiah 60:1-2.

These beautiful words from God are the reality that trumps what Christians sometimes see and feel. He tells us to rise up (from our oppression) because our Light has come! His glory is upon us, just as it was with Joseph when he was thrown into a pit by his brothers, sold as a slave, slandered and sent to prison—and also 13 years later when he rose overnight to be Pharaoh's right-hand man. God's glory is upon us, just as it was with Moses when he was humbled on the back side of the desert—and also 40 years later when he was exalted to lead the Israelites out of Egypt.

The glory of God is upon us in the midst of our hardship as well as in the day of our triumph. This is a truth we must believe and rely on. During the difficult times, we must praise and worship the Lord. Every day we must rise to a new life that is focused on pleasing Him. That's exactly what Moses and Joseph did, along with numerous others who've made a supernatural impact on this world.

Thank You, Lord, for choosing the lowly and the unimportant as recipients of Your grace. Thank You for giving us our own significant page in the history of Your kingdom.

_____

_____

_____

_____

_____

_____

_____

Glorious Grace

January 12, 2009

We've all heard that grace is "God's unmerited favor." That is certainly true, but grace goes quite a bit further—all the way to "amazing." Grace is found in every promise of God to do for us what we're incapable of doing for ourselves. With these glorious assurances, the Bible overflows.

My list of "humanly improbable" and "clearly impossible" needs is growing, so grace is exactly what I need. Oh, yes! I'll take an extra-large serving! And what about you? What do you need that only God can provide? What has the Lord been whispering to your heart? What will you have faith for?

I believe the entire body of Christ is moving into a period of increased and unprecedented grace. This will be visible to the unsaved world and will draw them into salvation—into God's kingdom of never-ending glory.

To prepare for glory, both now and in the future, we must sanctify our bodies, minds and spirits. (Please don't worry. Grace is always waiting, more than ready to help.)

And Joshua said to the people, "Sanctify yourselves, for tomorrow the Lord will do wonders among you" – Joshua 3:5.

Remember, we're God's representatives. Through us, He wants to show the world what He yearns to do for them. The world is in for a big surprise, and so are many Christians. Change is certainly coming, and it will be better than we imagine (1 Corinthians 2:9).

For the Lord God is a sun and shield; the Lord will give grace and glory; no good thing will He withhold from those who walk uprightly - Psalm 84:11.

Lord, we thank You for the grace that surrounds us every day. With much anticipation, we await the flood of increased grace that is coming our way. Hope is dancing within our hearts. We find ourselves loving You more than ever!

Pray For Grace

November 23, 2012

Surely He shall deliver you from the snare of the fowler ...He shall cover you with His feathers, and under His wings you shall take refuge... - Psalm 91:3-4.

It happens to all of us. We get blind-sided by words or actions that push our emotional buttons. Before we know it, we have responded poorly. The enemy sets many traps, and sometimes we are caught. And, no matter what type of sin, we know right away that we've "messed up" because the Spirit within us is grieved. We quickly confess our sin, we're forgiven by God, and we make amends as He leads.

However, the enemy doesn't want to let us off the hook. Those trouble-making demons try to make us squirm and fret and feel ashamed. They want our misdemeanors to be front-page news. God merely wants us to repent, but the demonic realm tries to make us *pay*.

Too many times I've fallen for this demand of the enemy—that I feel like a failure and be troubled over the fallout of my error. But the day came when my growing wisdom was sufficient to break the cycle. Time spent in the presence of God made me bold enough to think that He would "cover for me." Since Jesus' blood paid for my sin, then I would expect His grace to lift me above any condemnation.

It wasn't long before the next malfunction occurred. But now I could see my human failure as an opportunity. I began to test my new boldness by asking the Lord to stand in the gap for me—to take up the slack of my weakness and help me grow in this area. And every time, my request has been satisfied! The problems quickly dissolve, and peace is restored.

God knows ahead of time when we're going to fail a test, but He puts us through the paces anyway. He wants us to know our weakness, so we will pray for His abundant grace. He's always waiting to give us refuge under His mighty wings.

Dear Lord, we thank You for Your grace from the bottom of our hearts. We would be in serious trouble without it. Please help us impart Your grace to the world around us, just as we have received it from You.

Stewards of Grace

December 15, 2012

I do not set aside the grace of God; for if righteousness comes through the law, then Christ died in vain – Galatians 2:21.

The longer I live, the more I see the tremendous value of grace. When first hearing of it, I claimed this gift for myself. Then, as I matured, God opened my eyes to see the need in others to be met with grace instead of the law. Judgement is cold and harsh, while grace is bright, warm and full of life. Grace is the favor of God that shines a light and "makes a way" for all who turn to Him in their weakness. Grace gives us dynamic hope and inspires us to look for the glory of God right here on earth.

Let us therefore come boldly to the throne of grace, that we may obtain mercy and find grace to help in time of need – Hebrews 4:16.

As human need increases in this world, the value of grace increases even more. Today we are faced with abuse of governmental power, failing economy, moral decay, and widespread destruction. But grace is fully prepared to conquer these evil strongholds. Grace is always ready when believers stand in the gap to intercede.

Christians are called to be stewards of God's grace, and this requires loosing it through prayer. Whether petitioning for the lost or for other Christians, when we ask for mercy instead of judgement, then we're effectively sending grace into the world.

Grace is enthroned within God's heart. It invites us to rise by faith and enter His presence. We can freely partake of His mercy and grace whenever we need it. *How absolutely amazing!*

Grace always calls the sinner to step higher. It paves a way for repentance. When the Holy Spirit leads us to intercede and call for saving grace, it's for those who will respond one day and enter God's high ground of righteousness.

Grace is longsuffering. An unsaved sinner's need for grace can last a lifetime, right up to the hour of their departure. But when grace is prescribed by God, it does not fail. Intercessors must be willing to travel a long and rocky road.

Grace opens doors that have been locked. Our prayer for grace releases God's power at the scene of human struggle. Doors swing open, waters part, and mountains begin to crumble.

Grace clears the way for destiny and glory. Residing in the breath of God's word, grace blows away every deception and entrapment. It creates an atmosphere for greatness.

Oh, how I love this amazing grace! First it brings us to the loving arms of God (Ephesians 2:8), then every day thereafter it surrounds us with the sturdy shield of His favor (Psalm 5:12). Grace offers significant destiny to all who will respond (2 Timothy 1:9). Grace is big, fat, wide and strong, reaching throughout eternity (Psalm 103:17). Such a gift is meant to be held in the highest esteem. It should be carefully guarded but never hidden away. This treasure is meant to be shared.

Dear Lord, we thank You for Your ever-present gift of grace. Let the whole world watch as Your wondrous favor dances into dark places, lifting high the light of Your word and singing joyfully of Your love.

_____

_____

_____

_____

_____

_____

_____

_____

_____

_____

From the Day We're Born

April 28, 2008

Christians are recipients of grace from the day we're born. Before salvation, we're generally unaware of God's favor. But even so, He broods over us like a mother hen; teaching, nurturing and leading us to safety. When the sailing of life is smooth, we may think we're lucky or even deserving of what comes our way—never suspecting that grace has wrapped its arms around us—not even knowing what grace is. Even the turbulent seas we encounter are a form of grace that brings us to our knees before the Lord.

Through salvation and sanctification, we begin to see our utter helplessness and our need for God. Yes, after salvation we're even *more* aware of our poverty apart from Him. We find that we're unable to do anything good without the indwelling life of God. As the transformation continues, our self-confidence crumbles further. The day arrives when we cast ourselves entirely on the mercy and grace of the Lord. Finally! We know that we're wretched without Him.

Knowing our critical need for God is a very good thing. Now, with every step, we'll lean upon Him with all of our weight, knowing that we're supported and dearly loved.

"'Twas grace that taught my heart to fear, and grace my fears relieved." These words by John Newton are beloved and enduring because they are so very true.

But by the grace of God I am what I am, and His grace toward me was not in vain; but I labored more abundantly than they all, yet not I, but the grace of God which was with me -
1 Corinthians 15:10.

Oh, how sweet is the touch of Your grace, dear Lord! Just a stroke of Your little finger puts our hearts in alignment with You. Without Your grace, we could not face the challenges of the day, but with it, we climb mountains.

_____

_____

A World of Grace & Miracles

October 5, 2014

He who observes the wind will not sow, and he who regards the clouds will not reap – Ecclesiastes 11:4.

The reality of God's presence and power is not always at the forefront of our minds. We take for granted that the sun will rise, and rain will fall. We often forget that God is the sustaining force behind these wondrous events. But as Christians are moved from glory to glory, our faith expands, and we're more in tune with the proximity of God and all that He is. Our faith rests firmly on His loving, holy character—upon His willingness to do whatever it takes to advance His kingdom and redeem what was lost in the fall.

God upholds the laws of nature that He has put into place, but His grace overrides these laws when miracles are needed. At Joshua's prophetic command, God caused the sun and the moon to stand still until Israel had defeated its enemies (Joshua 10:12-13). Why wouldn't He also cure a serious illness or even raise the dead? Why wouldn't He provide all that is needed to support the destinies He has given us? He does, in fact, do *all* these things today!

He who did not spare His own Son, but delivered Him up for us all, how shall He not with Him also freely give us all things? – Romans 8:32.

I've heard it said that one miracle is worth a thousand sermons, and I completely agree. The lifelong impact of a supernatural event cannot be measured. Seeing someone dramatically healed or observing a life set free from habitual sin is enough to awaken a slumbering soul.

Do you want to see God's grace outweigh the natural laws in your own life? Then sow some seeds of faith today. Refrain from "observing the wind" and "regarding the clouds." Don't miss the wonders that God has reserved especially for you.

Dear Lord, please don't let us take You for granted. Don't let us miss a single drop of Your glorious grace. Remind us of Your zeal to redeem and restore so we won't neglect to pray. Please help us to believe.

Great Expectation

July 23, 2009

By faith we see the grace and glory of God unfold—warmly, richly, perfectly. His love blooms in every corner of our domains when we rest in Him and trust Him with the costly seed we've sown. Some of this seed will take years to germinate, provoking many tears and requiring countless hours of prayer. But God is faithful to respond:

If you abide in Me, and My words abide in you, you will ask what you desire, and it shall be done for you – John 15:7.

Today, the overwhelming grace and glory of the Lord is rising up like mighty ocean waves, pushing steadily toward our shores. We must scan the horizon with great expectation, setting aside all trust in human schemes, as we watch for God's supernatural blessing to appear.

And God is able to make all grace abound to you, so that having all sufficiency in all things at all times, you may abound in every good work – 2 Corinthians 9:8 ESV.

Thank You, Lord, for the works of Your heart and hands. Thank You for the joy of life as it flourishes in Your holy care. We praise You, Lord, for Your steadfast love that seeks and saves the lost—that sanctifies and empowers Your kingdom here on Earth.

_____

_____

_____

_____

_____

_____

_____

THE WORD

Reaching Deep

August 14, 2007

...blessed are those who trust in the LORD and have made the LORD their hope and confidence. They are like trees planted along a riverbank, with roots that reach deep into the water. Such trees are not bothered by the heat or worried by long months of drought. Their leaves stay green, and they go right on producing delicious fruit - Jeremiah 17:7-8 NLT.

Only faith will cause our roots to reach for something we cannot see. And only faith will *keep* us reaching until we tap into the deepest reservoir—the living water that quenches every terrible thirst.

Lengthy spiritual trials will stir up and strengthen our faith. They give us prolonged need for water and urge our roots to grow increasingly deep. Then, when a widespread drought is in the land, we already have access to hidden water. Our long, vertical roots will also hold us steady when fierce winds blow. We'll stand up tall and strong, with no danger of toppling over.

To cooperate with the Lord in our own "deepening" process, we must consistently read His word and listen for His voice. Let's not tarry or be distracted in our search for living water. To be victorious tomorrow, we must tap into our source today.

And he showed me a pure river of water of life, clear as crystal, proceeding from the throne of God and of the Lamb – Revelation 22:1.

In times of drought, dear Lord, You are a constant, faithful source. Being planted on the banks of Your river is a privilege and a joy. Your clear, pure water gives us life and produces excellent fruit. We thank You for every drop.

_____

_____

_____

Thirst

June 7, 2007

White-tailed deer are plentiful in rural Georgia, and I often see hoof prints to remind me of their presence. But recently they've become more visible. A two-month drought is causing the deer to move around in search of water and edible foliage. I woke one morning last week to find a doe and two young bucks in my yard. I even saw one in mid-afternoon, walking toward the tub of fresh water that I keep near the edge of the woods. The deer's need for refreshment outweighs the heightened risk they take.

Our lives, both physical and spiritual, depend upon drinking the fresh, clean water of the Word. If this no longer flows at our usual watering place, then we must rise up and go after it, searching both night and day, until we find it.

Purity is vital. We all know that water is much healthier to drink than carbonated beverages with their unnatural ingredients. Likewise, the purity of the Word is better than the polluted substitutes of this world. Let's not get hooked on something that will slowly poison us. Instead, let's drink living water from the holy river of God.

Jesus answered and said to her, "If you knew the gift of God, and who it is who says to you, 'Give Me a drink,' you would have asked Him, and He would have given you living water" - John 4:10.

As the Word, dear Lord, You pursue our "thirsty places" that are most in need of help. You wash our feverish hearts with waves of cooling revelation. You bring refreshment and revival to all who will partake. We thank You for giving us life.

_____

_____

_____

_____

_____

Life and Health

November 15, 2009

My son, give attention to my words; incline your ear to my sayings. Do not let them depart from your eyes; keep them in the midst of your heart; for they are life to those who find them, and health to all their flesh - Proverbs 4:20-22.

The Word is wisdom and understanding to all who will hear it. Pure and powerful, it is literally *life* and *health* to everyone who reads it and earnestly receives it. Through the Word, we can actually partake of the life of God—the beating of His holy heart and the sustenance of His breath. We can love as He loves and live as He lives.

The dynamic Word will always expand to meet our growing capacity for truth. Precept upon precept, the Word responds to our needs, and it also satisfies God's holy purpose. With every new day, the Word extends bountiful grace to each who will "give their attention" and "incline their ears."

Thank You, Lord, for giving Yourself to us through the Word. Thank You for revealing Your heart, Your mind and Your Spirit for us to freely feast upon. Help us to be good stewards of all that we obtain.

_____

_____

_____

_____

_____

_____

_____

_____

_____

The Voice of the Lord

September 27, 2010

The voice of the Lord is over the waters; the God of glory thunders; the Lord is over many waters. The voice of the Lord is powerful; the voice of the Lord is full of majesty. The voice of the Lord breaks the cedars, yes, the Lord splinters the cedars of Lebanon. He makes them also skip like a calf, Lebanon and Sirion like a young wild ox. The voice of the Lord divides the flames of fire. The voice of the Lord shakes the wilderness... - Psalm 29:3-8.

David composed and sang this psalm about God's voice while he was watching a violent storm—probably from a mountain cave during his time of exile. David was in awe. The tempest around him was an audio-visual showcase of God's power. But the awe that David felt was not due to the raging display. It was because of who it represented. When writing about "the voice of the Lord," David knew the God of whom he wrote. He knew the God who spoke.

David understood that the violent storm was a display with holy purpose. Through the elements of nature, God clearly revealed the power in His voice. Whenever He proclaims His will, this power is released and great things happen.

For He spoke, and it was done; He commanded, and it stood fast - Psalm 33:9.

What the Lord showed David almost 3000 years ago was recorded for us to see today. But the spiritual lesson is only perceived by those who are ready—to those who are ever mindful that Christians are the dwelling place of our holy God. His voice through our lips can create a tempest in the spiritual realm, just like the one that David observed from his cave. If we proclaim God's will, then towering obstacles will splinter before us, just like "the cedars of Lebanon." Mountains will meekly step aside. Any wilderness in the years ahead will "shake" at the sound of the Word, when it's spoken by us with authority.

The Lord will give [unyielding and impenetrable] strength to His people; the Lord will bless His people with peace – Psalm 29:11 AMPC.

Today, let us be instruments of God, proclaiming truth, life, and peace over every person we know and every situation we face. When released with faith, the strength of God's voice from our lips will be felt throughout the world. Yes! Let the Word go forth!

Dear Lord, Your displays of strength are inspiring! As we read Your word, our fainting hearts are revived. Your Spirit speaks and we are blessed with peace. Your Spirit speaks again, and we are filled with purpose and power.

The Word is God

January 19, 2010

Sometimes, when I get accustomed to hearing from the Lord in a particular way, He proceeds to "change the channel." Then I have to find Him in a new place. And sometimes, just when I start to feel comfortably close, He moves to the left or the right, requiring that I seek Him with more determination—or so it seems. God stretches and expands us in mysterious ways which we often don't understand. But if we love Him, we continue to follow and reach for more. Our hearts are entwined with His, so we can't be apart for long or endure much distance.

The Lord can be perplexing at times, but we always have the Word as our constant, guiding light. We must never forget that the Word *is* God, and we can have as much of Him as we desire.

In the beginning was the Word, and the Word was with God, and the Word was God – John 1:1.

The Word will speak to us wherever we stand—on a bright hill of mature understanding or in a dark valley of confusion. The Word will flow in us like blood, carrying life to every hidden part. The Word is alive with love, revelation, and power. If we treat the Word as the living presence of God instead of a compilation of facts to be remembered, then we'll be blessed with glorious interaction.

Then Jesus said to those Jews who believed Him, "If you abide in My word, you are My disciples indeed" – John 8:31.

Any activity that consistently displaces the reading of scripture should be considered an idol. But if we spend time in the Word each day, placing it above all else, then we are disciples indeed.

If you abide in Me, and My words abide in you, you will ask what you desire, and it shall be done for you – John 15:7.

Abiding—asking—receiving. Now that's an excellent deal!

Dear Lord, please help us mine the depths of Your word. Let Your Spirit guide us and teach us. Let Your word take root within us and never depart. Let it blossom, bear fruit, and scatter seed wherever we go.

_____

_____

_____

_____

_____

_____

_____

_____

_____

_____

_____

_____

_____

_____

_____

_____

_____

_____

_____

The Sword of the Spirit

January 8, 2012

And take...the sword of the Spirit, which is the word of God – Ephesians 6:17.

Let's make no mistake. Prayer *is* spiritual warfare. When Christians step onto this battlefield, we must be heavily armed. The sword of the Spirit—the word of God—is our matchless, overpowering weapon. It cannot be defeated.

For years, I prayed without much power. I would ask God to "please teach Mary Anne" or to "please make Julia stop behaving badly." I'm sure my prayers were heard in Heaven, but they lacked the mighty breath of God that is found in scripture. Demons were probably mocking my words because they carried no authority. But now I use the word of God when I pray. This often stirs up a hornet's nest of backlash and strong defiance from Satan's camp. Demons are hoping that I'll shut up and go away. However, the enemy has to obey God's word if I insist. And I *do* insist. I know the Word, and I believe it. I proclaim it boldly in prayer. Every day, I wield the sword of the Spirit and enforce the will of God. Change is taking place.

It is the will of God that no one should perish. When praying for friends and family I declare for each that "You shall live and not die" (Psalm 18:17). I assert that "No weapon formed against you will prosper" (Isaiah 54:17). When I see a need for enlightenment, I proclaim that God will send "the Spirit of wisdom and revelation in the knowledge of Him" (Ephesians 1:17).

Using God's word, Christians can break Satan's hold on those we love. Like waves upon a shore, we can demolish the strongholds of darkness with a relentless pounding of light and truth. Our sword from the Most High God has preeminent power, so we must use it every day, at every opportunity. This takes commitment and effort, but excellent results are guaranteed.

For as the rain comes down, and the snow from heaven, and do not return there, but water the earth, and make it bring forth and bud, that it may give seed to the sower and bread to the eater,

so shall My word be that goes forth from My mouth; it shall not return to Me void, but it shall accomplish what I please, and it shall prosper in the thing for which I sent it - Isaiah 55:10-11.

We thank You, Lord, for arming us with a sharp and gleaming sword. With it, we will enforce Jesus' victory at the cross. We will bring the Father's will from Heaven to Earth.

_____

_____

_____

_____

_____

_____

_____

_____

_____

_____

_____

_____

_____

_____

_____

_____

_____

_____

The Power of the Word

November 4, 2012

Circumstances can be daunting, but in the hand of God, they're fuel for His refining fire. While the enemy tries to crush the life out of us, the Lord is concurrently fine-tuning us with the very same conditions. The demonic realm is Hell-bent on convincing us that our hope is in vain and all is lost, but the Spirit tells us to *"Arise, shine; for your light has come!" (Isaiah 60:1)*.

The enemy loves to hit us hard (cruel words will suffice), then quickly hit us a second time (a miserable illness will do), then hit us again (unexpected bills are never welcome), and *again* (the "difficult person" in our life decides to kick it up a notch). These combined attacks have an exponential effect. In our weakened state, frightening, tormenting thoughts will assail our minds: *"God has said for years that things will change, but nothing is any different—and you have yourself to blame for that. The truth is, things will get much worse. You just wait and see."*

Then the Spirit of God will whisper, *"Don't be afraid. All is well. You won't be hurt because I'm in complete control. Just trust Me and obey."* And we are thinking, *"But God, these things do hurt, and I'm getting very tired. I'm not sure I can take this much longer."* With exceeding grace, the Spirit reminds us of relevant words, according to our specific need. He once gave me the following verse, revealing the goodness of God, effective *today*:

[What, what would have become of me] had I not believed that I would see the Lord's goodness in the land of the living – Psalm 27:13 AMPC.

"What would have become of me had I not believed..." This clearly reveals the importance of faith. And gloriously, the Word holds unlimited power to increase our trust in God. It gives us practical instruction while assuring us of glorious victory with the Lord at our side. The Word also imparts a strong responsibility to accept and obey its message of hope.

Wait and hope for and expect the Lord; be brave and of good courage and let your heart be stout and enduring. Yes, wait for and hope for and expect the Lord – Psalm 27:14 AMPC.

I love the concluding lines of Psalm 27 in the Amplified Classic Bible. This version adds the word "expect" to present a full, rich meaning. God is telling us to actively anticipate His answers to our prayers (when they align with His will). He's telling us to "watch our mailbox" for the delivery of every promise that He's whispered in our ears. No matter what our circumstances imply, we're told to have great expectation of our faithful Lord.

Thank You, God, for the power of Your words to make us "brave and of good courage." When they're applied by Your Spirit, our hearts become "stout and enduring." We praise You, Lord, for Your refining fire and Your total commitment to transform us. Help us to never faint, but to always anticipate Your goodness. Help us to always believe.

It Is Settled

February 20, 2011

Forever, O Lord, Your word is settled in heaven. Your faithfulness endures to all generations; You established the earth, and it abides - Psalm 119:89-90.

Psalm 119 is the longest chapter in the Bible. Within its span, much is declared, but I see two key principles rising to the surface: The value of the Word—and God's faithfulness to uphold and perform it. The stability and success of every Christian life hinges upon our belief in those two things.

Have you received a promise from the Lord about a matter that is dear to your heart? If so, this personal pledge will powerfully sustain you through valleys, floods, and fire while you wait for it to manifest. The amazing power of a promise from God stems from the two elements found in Psalm 119—from the integrity of His word (either scripture or a communication from Him that fully aligns with scripture) and from the faithfulness of His being.

Because Satan has limited power, he relies heavily on trickery to induce harm, just as with Eve, when he cast doubt on God's word and on His character:

Now the serpent was more cunning than any beast of the field which the LORD God had made. And he said to the woman, "Has God indeed said, 'You shall not eat of every tree of the garden'?" - Genesis 3:1.

"Did God really tell you that? Maybe you imagined those words. Maybe you misunderstood Him. Does God even care about the situation?" Every day the enemy hints that my hearing is faulty, or that God is not to be trusted. The powers of darkness know that faith is the key to fulfillment of a promise, so attempts to steal that key will be relentless.

Whenever stricken with doubt, we should go immediately to the Lord to ask for confirmation of His word. I've been waiting quite a while for one particular promise to take shape. I've asked for verification many times because the issue is of major importance. The enemy taunts me daily, but God has been faithful to encourage and reassure me. No matter how often I ask for confirmation of His promise, He lovingly answers. One memorable response was His quoting of scripture to me: *"Am I a man that I should lie?"* At first, I thought this was a rebuke, but then I realized that God was describing His character. He was reminding me that He is faithful—that I can rely on Him:

God is not man, that he should lie, or a son of man, that he should change his mind. Has he said, and will he not do it? Or has he spoken, and will he not fulfill it? – Numbers 23:19 ESV.

Once God speaks, then the matter is settled. He never breaks His promises or changes His mind as humans do. Our trust in His word and His character equips us to change the world.

Thank You, Lord, for speaking so clearly. Please help us believe every beautiful word from Your mouth. Help us to lean completely on Your faithfulness.

_____

_____

_____

_____

_____

_____

_____

_____

_____

_____

_____

HEARING THE VOICE OF GOD

One Word from God

September 22, 2008

I'm convinced that we hear from the Lord more frequently if we put value on what He's already said. Whenever He speaks to me, I promptly write it down. Then if the enemy distracts me from a message, I'll find it later and be reminded. One word from God has power to change my life or the lives of others, and I don't want to lose track of it.

The Lord has a passion to talk with each one of us, but He communicates on His terms, not ours—requiring the utmost respect. Christian ears may become deaf to God's voice if previous words have been lightly esteemed or totally ignored.

Some churchgoers are steeped in knowledge from the Bible, but they don't feel the need for personal words from the Spirit of God. They effectively keep Him at a distance by only receiving words of general application. Knowledge is a precious gift, but it must be applied with relevance to each situation we face. If we don't seek personal direction, then we're pridefully leaning on our own understanding (Proverbs 3:5).

Now is the time to seek the voice of the Lord! Let's humbly ask Him to open our ears, then listen with a heart that is willing to obey and ready to be amazed.

Morning by morning he wakens me and opens my understanding to his will. The Sovereign Lord has spoken to me, and I have listened. I have not rebelled or turned away - Isaiah 50:4-5 NLT.

Please protect us from our own reasoning, Lord. Guard us from the voices of this world. Let our understanding come only from You—that we may live (Psalm 119:144). Please remove any obstruction from our ears. We want to hear when You whisper.

Revelation

October 28, 2012

Therefore I...do not cease to give thanks for you, making mention of you in my prayers: that the God of our Lord Jesus Christ, the Father of glory, may give to you the spirit of wisdom and revelation in the knowledge of Him... - Ephesians 1:15-17.

Revelation from God comes to us in many forms. We're presented with vivid dreams and detailed visions.* Words and ideas are spoken to us by the Spirit within. As we read the Bible, the Lord will sometimes quicken His word so it speaks to us on a personal level.

We're given revelation for a number of reasons. It may come as a warning, or as edification, insight, and encouragement. It goes without saying that when God speaks, we should listen carefully and respond properly. Anything less is arrogant and reckless.

In whatever form the revelations come and for whatever purpose they are sent, it's critical that we incorporate them in our prayer. Any impending danger disclosed by God should obviously be prayed against. Everything else is a reflection of His heart and mind—an unveiling of His will. Whenever we know God's will, we should pray that it comes to pass.

The Lord loves to reveal what we need to know.

During a recent one-week vacation, I saw seven rainbows. I thought this was unusual, and I felt that my seeing them was significant. Using an online concordance, I searched for scripture about rainbows. I found the familiar verses about God's covenant with man. Then I was surprised by a wonderful verse that was entirely new to me:

**Like the appearance of a rainbow in a cloud on a rainy day, so was the appearance of the brightness all around it. This was the appearance of the likeness of the glory of the LORD –
Ezekiel 1:28.**

Through seven rainbows and a corresponding scripture, God revealed His glory to me. He showed me that I am covered and surrounded by it.

Because of this new insight, I now pray for God's glory to enter situations or certain areas or even a person's heart.

On this same week of vacation, I met a Christian couple on the beach. We talked for a while and ended up praying together. During our prayer, God gave the woman a vision about someone I love. She shared it with me, and now I use this new revelation in my prayers of intercession. This divine appointment supplied me with a sharp new weapon.

If you're not getting as much revelation from the Lord as you want, then start praying that you will. Claiming the words of Ephesians 1:15-21 for yourself is an excellent place to begin. When your spiritual hearing starts to increase, be sure to follow through with praise, prayer and obedience.

Thank You, Lord, for Your generous Spirit of wisdom and revelation. Personal communication with You is empowering and essential for victory in Your kingdom. Please pour Your grace upon us without restraint. Help us to always respond in action and in prayer according to Your will.

* The visions I refer to in this book are the mental images God gives us during times of prayer. After some time of worship, I simply ask, "Lord, what is on Your mind to show me today?" He almost always responds with a visual message, sometimes even before I ask.

_____

_____

_____

_____

_____

_____

_____

_____

_____

Dreams

January 16, 2006

God still speaks to His people in dreams. When we believe that this will actually happen to *us*, then we'll begin to reap the rewards. These nocturnal messages offer encouragement, direction, correction and sometimes warning.

Then, being divinely warned in a dream that they should not return to Herod, they departed for their own country another way – Matthew 2:12.

Not every dream is from God, but if we're pursuing a close relationship with Him, we can expect that He will sometimes talk to us at night when we're not distracted by daily activity and by our own thoughts. Within the boundaries of a dream, God has our undivided attention.

Dreams are soon forgotten, so I suggest that you record every detail, from beginning to end, as soon as you wake.

We can often interpret our own dreams. Some of the images will be unique to our personal experience, so that will help with our discernment. And the components we don't immediately understand will be explained by God if we ask Him. He may respond immediately, but He will sometimes wait until the time is right. Enlightenment will come in a variety of ways—maybe in the context of an upcoming event—maybe during a conversation, or maybe while reading the Word. We can always count on God to shine His light where it's needed.

Because the body of Christ works together, some Christians have been gifted as interpreters of dreams, and they can help reveal the deeply hidden truths. However, certain dream symbols are universal, and these can be learned from Christian experts on the subject.*

Please take a step of faith tonight. Before you go to sleep, invite the Lord to reveal Himself in your dreams. Ask Him to show you what's on His mind.

It's exciting, Lord, to wake in the morning and realize that You have spoken during the night. We ask that You do this more often. Every communication from You is a gift that we treasure.

* I like "Illustrated Dictionary of Dream Symbols" by Dr. Joe Ibojie.

_____

_____

_____

_____

_____

_____

_____

_____

_____

_____

_____

_____

_____

_____

_____

_____

_____

_____

Communication

December 11, 2010

Held within God's word are so many promises! Christians should always be looking for good to come their way. In spite of this, the enemy tries to convince us that "now is not the time" or that "these words don't apply to us today." Demonic warnings to "not get our hopes up" will subtly infiltrate our thoughts. Countering this attack, the Holy Spirit speaks to us individually, giving us personal visions of the future and conferring promises that have our names engraved on them. These messages will never contradict scripture. Instead, they magnify the Word by giving it specific form, power and personality.

Now here is a critical truth relating to promises: We *must* hear God's voice and receive His vision for us. To obtain personal assurance for today along with a clear map to our destiny, then close interaction with the Lord is required. If we don't communicate with Him, then we won't anticipate or receive what He wants to give us.

I cannot count the times that God has said to me, *"Relax. Don't worry. I see what's going on. Give it to Me, then trust Me to handle it."* These comforting words of assurance get me through the rigors of daily living, but my favorite communication is the kind that causes me to look ahead:

- Many years ago, God told me to *"Write. Just keep writing."* Those words are not in the Bible, but they are in the heart and mind of the Lord for me. His direction to write came with a guarantee that He would help and inspire me. I look ahead with excitement regarding the destiny of these written words.

- The Lord has given me valuable insight concerning the people I love. Because of this, I can pray with confidence and with tactical precision, always looking forward to their salvation and the fulfillment of their destiny.

- I have received personal promises about my future that have kept me afloat on some dark and stormy seas. These peeks into the years ahead bring powerful hope.

Now what about you? Are you holding tightly to a word or a vision? Do you anticipate the glory of days ahead? Are you filled with expectation, waiting for promises to unfold?

Remember Your promise to me; it is my only hope. Your promise revives me; it comforts me in all my troubles - Psalm 119:49-50 NLT.

If your "only hope" is a personal pledge from God, then you live in a place of great favor. You are enriched every day that you wait on the Lord, and you'll be blessed beyond your expectations when His promise arrives.

Thank You, Lord, for Your precious promises. Thank You for backing them up with Your faithfulness and supporting them with Your love. Interacting with You is exciting, and waiting on You is an honor.

_____

_____

_____

_____

_____

_____

_____

_____

_____

_____

_____

Walking on Water

April 15, 2015

Quite often, the Lord speaks to me early in the morning while I lay awake in bed, waiting for the alarm to sound. He gives me His wonderful, insightful thoughts on important matters at hand. Recently, He brought up the subject of walking on water. *"That's what I'm asking you to do,"* He said. Then He turned my thoughts to His disciple, Peter:

And Peter answered Him and said, "Lord, if it is You, command me to come to You on the water." So He said, "Come" – Matthew 14:28.

I thought of how this passionate man leapt from the boat to walk toward Jesus, but then he noticed the wind and the waves and began to sink (Matthew 14:25-33). While I was empathizing with Peter's conflicting emotions, the Spirit reminded me of a well-known scripture:

Have I not commanded you? Be strong and of good courage; do not be afraid, nor be dismayed, for the LORD your God is with you wherever you go – Joshua 1:9.

Still in bed but wide awake, I was thinking, *"Yes! This is how I will live. I'll walk on water! I won't be afraid."* God was certainly starting my day on a positive and challenging note. But He wasn't finished yet. He topped off His inspiring words by revealing that the acronym for "walk on water" is WOW! That couldn't possibly be more fitting.

Throughout the day, I thought of my morning interaction with the Lord. Essentially, He had said to me, *"Yes, Susan, you can trust that it's My voice you've been hearing. I know that believing My promise has stretched your faith considerably, and it has taken you far out of your comfort zone. But I don't want you to be anxious. As you step out onto the water, just keep your eyes on Me."*

I can't share the details of what I'm believing for, but I know my situation is common to man. Therefore, God's message to me is also for you. Walking on water is something that sooner or later, we're all asked to do. It will be a situation or a task that, apart from God, we cannot handle successfully. It may be a "perfect storm" of converging events. Or it may be a fairly minor situation that, to you, is simply intolerable.

It's important to understand that walking on water can never be done in human strength. God will let us try, if only to show us our inability. Ultimately, we must cry out to Him for an increase of faith and of courage.

...looking unto Jesus, the author and finisher of our faith... - Hebrews 12:2.

So, what is God requiring of you? What body of water is He asking you to walk upon in faith? Are you still in the process of discovering your helplessness, or have you moved onward to a place of appealing to God for help? Remember that when you're called to step out of the boat, the outstretched arms of Jesus are always there to hold you up.

Christian growth can be frightening, Lord, but through the trials, we learn of Your strength and Your faithfulness. As we lean on You, we discover more depths of Your love. We learn of Your compassion for our frailty. With every passing day, You become more dear to us.

Prophetic Prayer

April 15, 2012

Now to Him who is able to do exceedingly abundantly above all that we ask or think, according to the power that works in us, to Him be glory in the church by Christ Jesus to all generations, forever and ever. Amen – Ephesians 3:20-21.

Many of us get caught up in the words "exceedingly abundantly above all that we ask or think"—and for good cause. In light of our needy condition, God's power and grace are exciting to think about. But with our focus squarely on God's greatness, we might not absorb the next string of words. Our Lord works "exceedingly abundantly above all that we ask or think—*according to the power that works in us..."*

Did you catch that? *According to the power that works in us!* These words echo the meaning of another well-known verse:

To them God willed to make known what are the riches of the glory of this mystery among the Gentiles: which is Christ in you, the hope of glory - Colossians 1:27.

The message of God's power flowing through weak human vessels has always been close to my heart. The Lord reminds me of it quite often because it's essential to His purpose for my life. His most recent reminder was just a few days ago. The Holy Spirit spoke clearly into my mind, but instead of distinct words, He gave me a distinct thought. Here is my paraphrase of the message:

> *I'm your Friend, and we're united in purpose. I want to prophesy My will through you so it will come to pass.*

This message sounds rather general, but the Spirit gave me understanding that I should "pray prophetically" over my two most pressing needs. I should proclaim every relevant scripture and every personal word from God that comes to mind regarding these matters. Wow! What a way to start my day. Two locked doors will soon swing open! God has given me the key.

To pray prophetically is an excellent way to connect and engage with the Hope of Glory residing within us.

Praying prophetically does require a healthy level of faith in who God is and what is in His heart. It's our faith that unleashes the truth and power within His words. But even if you're a "babe in Christ," don't let that keep you from trying. One of the best ways to build up faith is watching God respond to prayer.

Thank You, Lord, for including us in Your wonderful work. Thank You for building our faith so we can effectively use the sword of prophetic prayer. Please sanctify our hearts and our mouths, then let Your proclamations flow through us freely and often.

_____

_____

_____

_____

_____

_____

_____

_____

_____

_____

_____

_____

A Powerful Weapon

August 23, 2006

I came home one afternoon to find a black snake draped through the center of a large shrub near my front door. This was the only snake I've seen while living in my Georgia country home. First, I grabbed my camera and took several pictures. Then I used a broom to push at the intruder, hoping it would streak across the yard. Instead, it slithered out of site, deep within the shadows of the leafy Lantana bush.

Using the internet to identify the snake as a "southern black racer," I learned that it wasn't venomous. Racers eat plenty of mice, but also birds and their eggs. Now I was worried about the little Carolina Wrens that recently fledged from their nest in my garage. They were learning to catch the bugs that are drawn to this flowering shrub. Along with the wrens, several hummingbirds visit this plant throughout the day to sip from the blooms!

I went right away to a hardware store to buy some snake repellant—a smelly combination of mothball ingredients and Sulphur. I sprinkled this into all of the bushes around my house, and I haven't seen the reptile again.

Later in the week I was sitting at my computer, looking at digital photos of the snake. I thought of the threat this stealthy creature had been to the birds, and I remembered how the mixture of pungent chemicals caused the snake to leave. At this point, God interjected His thoughts, making a comparison between the snake in the bush and the spiritual enemies I've been fighting. He finished up by saying, *"Just as the smell of mothballs and Sulphur repelled the snake, the scent of praise will drive away your enemies."*

Think about that! To our spiritual enemies, the "scent of praise" becomes a repulsive stench. It is strong enough to make them leave. Believe me, after receiving this personal direction, complete with a visual aid, I will be praising God throughout the day for the rest of my life.

Now when they began to sing and to praise, the Lord set ambushes against the people of Ammon, Moab, and Mount Seir, who had come against Judah; and they were defeated –
2 Chronicles 20:22.

Your goodness is amazing, Lord. You go out of Your way to teach us, presenting truth that is paired with vivid illustrations. Please fill our hearts with praise for You, and let it pour forth extravagantly, just as You deserve.

_____

_____

_____

_____

_____

_____

_____

_____

_____

_____

_____

_____

_____

Building the Future

October 30, 2010

I'm always on the lookout for scripture to decree over my grandchildren, to build their future according to God's will. I also pray continuously for their parents; my daughter and her husband. These four people have an important place in the Kingdom of God, and I'm determined that they won't miss their destiny. Because I know the Lord agrees with me, I can pray for them with confidence.

One evening as I lay in bed, I asked God to give me a scripture to proclaim over my sweet little granddaughter. He responded immediately, telling me to pray that she will begin to "walk in the good works that He has prepared for her" (Ephesians 2:10). Knowing that I can depend on the Spirit for guidance in prayer and spiritual warfare is a blessing that boosts my confidence. I am not alone in the task of paving the way for these precious children.

The enemy works desperately hard to distract us, but God still holds us responsible to pray for our families. We closely witness their weakness and their needs, so we have the knowledge to pray specifically. During our prayer, we discover the intense longing of God for each one of them. This helps us to boldly pray without ceasing for everything they need.

Many waters cannot quench love; rivers cannot wash it away. If one were to give all the wealth of his house for love, it would be utterly scorned - Song of Solomon 8:7 NIV.

Christians have the heart and mind of Christ. We're endowed with a love that is supernatural and indestructible. When it's activated by faith, this tough, tenacious love works miracles.

Because the Lord has sanctified us, our prayers for family are heard. Because He loves us, they are answered.

Dear Lord, we thank You for giving us family to love and to fight for. They are the rich inheritance that You died on the cross to save. We thank You for the difficult ones. You've placed many prodigals into the prayerful care of parents and siblings who count it an honor to love them.

Songs of Deliverance

October 7, 2008

You are my hiding place; You shall preserve me from trouble; You shall surround me with songs of deliverance - Psalm 32:7.

The closer we get to God and the more we embrace His promises, then the more we'll meet resistance from the enemy. The troubles of this world will circle around us, trying to block our view of the Lord—of His loving protection and provision. It's true that our character is purified in difficult situations, and much fine-tuning will take place, but we still need divine encouragement to get through trying times.

I've recently suffered attacks from several directions, but I am blessed with supernatural peace. I know that God is in control. An interesting vision He gave me a couple weeks ago has brought me comfort amidst the turmoil:

> I was a palm tree—tall, healthy, and green. Hurricane wind was blowing hard against me. I withstood the fury of the wind and rain, but I was being splattered with bits of murky foam churned up by the roaring sea.

> I was concerned about the meaning of the foam, so I asked God to explain. He told me not to worry because even though I didn't like the mess and the insult of being splattered, this would not damage me in the least. Gentle rain would come to rinse it all away. Then He laughingly told me that no one has ever been hurt by sea foam.

Life can be challenging, but spending time with the Lord will give us clues about what is going on. This insight will keep us strong and even make us laugh as we weather the raging storm. "Songs of deliverance" will surround us and offer their gift of peace.

We love Your beautiful songs, dear Lord. They always bring good news—at just the right time, with delightfully perfect words. The voice of Your Spirit is cherished by all who hear.

51

Higher Ground

August 7, 2014

Happy is the man who finds wisdom, and the man who gains understanding; for her proceeds are better than the profits of silver, and her gain than fine gold.   She is more precious than rubies, and all the things you may desire cannot compare with her – Proverbs 3:13-15.

The Lord has recently given me a need for His divine strategy—for detailed instruction regarding a problem I face. Thankfully, He's trained me well in hearing His voice, so reception should not be a problem. I confidently expect to receive God's clear direction.

Since obtaining counsel from the Lord is critical for all of us, I want to share what I've learned.   I'm offering a casual list of precepts that will help any Christian move from a place of confusion to the higher ground of consistently hearing from God:

- To hear God's plan for victory—for today, next month or next year—submitting to Him is essential. This allows God to prepare you for increased understanding. Yield quickly to His methods of cleansing, healing and transformation. Humble yourself under His mighty hand, and He will exalt you in due time (1 Peter 5:6).

- First things first!   Understand that every majestic truth is preceded by an earlier foundational truth. Precept must be upon precept...line upon line...here a little, there a little (Isaiah 28:9-10). Getting to know God takes time. And you *must* know God to recognize His voice.

- Wisdom, understanding and knowledge—God will frequently speak through these (Proverbs 1:20-21).

- "Count it all joy" when trials arrive to test and strengthen your faith (James 1:2-8). Understand that tribulation brings greater need to hear God's voice and cause you to seek it fervently.

- While your faith is growing, take time to explore the numerous ways that God might speak to you. Listen for the many facets of His voice (John 10:4). Be persistent. Begin every day expecting to hear from the One who has plenty to say.

- Spend time in praise and worship. Increase your time in the Word. When you find the presence of God, you will naturally find His voice. Seek the Lord with all your heart and He will be found by you (Jeremiah 29:13).

- Practice obedience. God will only reveal His secrets when you can be trusted to use them well (Psalm 25:14).

- Know that God is on your side. He is the Way, the Truth and the Life (John 14:6). He wants you to succeed, and He will give you strategic help just as soon as you're ready.

My son, eat honey because it is good, and the honeycomb which is sweet to your taste; so shall the knowledge of wisdom be to your soul; if you have found it, there is a prospect, and your hope will not be cut off – Proverbs 24:13-14.

Dear Lord, we thank You for Your word and for Your Voice. Thank You for the beautifully narrow path that leads us to Your presence. Your sweet Spirit guides us always closer to the blessing that lies in You.

_____

_____

_____

_____

_____

_____

Great and Mighty Things

September 18, 2011

My annual Florida vacation had finally begun. While waiting for check-in time at my island condominium, I was walking along a bayside beach, photographing tropical birds. My attention was focused on an Egret, when I was approached by a man who asked, "Don't you want to photograph that rare horizontal rainbow?"

"Sure! Thanks a lot!" I had never seen or heard of a horizontal rainbow, but now I was photographing one. Just as the name implies, the rainbow was straight and flat. It was also very bright. The following week, I learned that the scientific name for this visual phenomenon is "circumhorizontal arc." These rainbows only form when plate-shaped ice crystals are present in cirrus clouds and when the sun is a certain distance from Earth. At some latitudes, they can never be seen.

Because I'm accustomed to the Lord speaking to me through nature, I thought this event might hold a personal message. I would have missed it entirely had it not been pointed out to me, so that in itself seemed significant—as if the message was hand delivered. I prayed for revelation of the meaning for me, and the Spirit of God soon answered:

> Scripture declares the rainbow to be a sign of covenant between God and the earth (Genesis 9:12, 13). In addition to God's original specific promise to never again cover the earth with a flood, I believe the rainbow symbolizes His intent to honor any covenant or promise He has made to His people, either corporately or individually. *It's a visual reminder from God that He keeps His promises.*

> The Spirit revealed to me that the unusual "horizontal" aspect of the rainbow was an important part of the message. Strong's Concordance presents to us the Greek word, "horizo" (3724). From "horizon," it means "to mark out or bound—to appoint, decree, specify—to declare, determine, limit, ordain."

> God was clearly saying to me, *"Susan, look up and see. My promise to you has been marked out. It has been specified, determined, ordained and decreed. My specific promise to you is "limited" (fitted) to My purpose for your life."*

<u>In a nutshell</u>: I should be greatly encouraged. God's promise to me is surely coming to pass, according to His purpose and at the predetermined time. He actually wrote this in the sky as a loving reminder.

I have shared this story with a goal in mind: I want you to *want* to hear God's voice. (If you don't care about hearing from the Lord, then you *won't*.) I want you to know that He has good news for you. I want you to believe that He has things to say about your future. If you're not hearing God's voice, then I want you to be jealous that He's speaking to me and not to you. I want you to chase after Him. (The truth is, if God will speak to me, then He will certainly speak to you.)

In my experience, God is the ultimate cheerleader. When I ask Him for encouragement, He quickly responds. But in the case of the horizontal rainbow, I didn't even have to ask. His beautiful sign in the sky was more like an a announcement. (Now *that's* exciting!)

No matter who you are or what you've done, the Lord will speak to you. Others' opinions of you don't matter to Him. God has purpose for you that is quite specific, and He's placed great potential within you. But you must have faith. You must believe that God will talk to you on a personal level. The fact that you're living and breathing is proof that your business on Earth isn't finished. Beginning today, you can start listening for God's voice. You can start receiving His direction. Just don't be surprised when you find yourself encouraged.

Call to Me, and I will answer you, and show you great and mighty things, which you do not know - Jeremiah 33:3.

Dear Lord, we love being involved in Your plans. Please keep our eyes and ears wide open so we can always receive Your direction. Keep our minds clear so we can accept every powerful word of encouragement. Lead us each day to relevant truth. Please prepare our hearts to be vessels of "great and mighty things."

Dessert Wine

May 15, 2010

I had a vivid dream that I'm sure is from the Lord. It applies directly to me, but it's also a clear picture of what God has for each member of the body of Christ—if you will receive it.

> <u>Dessert Wine</u>: I was sitting at a table set with fine white dishes and a white linen table cloth. The dinner was in progress. The food and the people were obscure, though I believe this was a gathering of my daughter's family and her in-laws. These people are Californians who often drink wine with meals, and the prominent matter in the dream was the wine on the table. I could see two bottles at my end of the table. They were identical brands with identical labels, but they were of different sizes. The large bottle was regular table wine, and the smaller bottle was a dessert wine. I was given the bottle of dessert wine. It was placed directly in front of me as my appointed drink.

God is the sweetest, richest Wine, and He is our appointed drink. The longer we know Him, the sweeter we perceive Him to be. The gifts from His heart and hands are also extremely sweet, coming always at the perfect time, with His blessing and for His purpose.

...“Every man at the beginning sets out the good wine, and when the guests have well drunk, then the inferior. You have kept the good wine until now!” – John 2:10.

Thank You, Lord, for being our Dessert Wine. First, You set a beautiful table before us, then Your presence transforms the meal to a special occasion—to a grand display of Your favor. We are exalted by the extravagance of Your love.

By the Work of His Hands

July 10, 2007

For since the creation of the world His invisible attributes are clearly seen, being understood by the things that are made, even His eternal power and Godhead, so that they are without excuse... - Romans 1:20.

When reading this scripture in the past, my focus has been on the message that "they are without excuse." But recently, while I was working on a nature photography project, the Holy Spirit said to me: *I will be known by the work of My hands.*

I soon realized that the Spirit had given me His modern paraphrase of Romans 1:20. And with the change of wording came a change of focus. "I will be known" resounded within me. God is taking my love for the beauty of nature to a higher level by telling me to look for revelation of Him in all that He has made.

I've often seen "lessons from God" in nature, and I've always known that creation reveals His traits and His personality. But now I'm being encouraged to pursue this path of awareness—to delve deeper into the heart of the Lord through the sound of rustling leaves, the touch of cool water, and the lofty flight of birds. I'm feeling exceedingly blessed by this invitation.

Let me exhort all of you to seek God in the same way. Spend time outdoors each day to browse through His portfolio. Look for reflection of our Lord in the glorious work of His hands.

Dear Lord, if nature is a hint of Your persona, then surely You are awesome! From the soulful song of a mourning dove to the piercing crack of a lightning bolt, Your voice cannot be missed. Feathers and flowers and pebbles and shells are expressions of Your love. You embrace with a breeze and beguile with the scent it carries. Creation worships all that You are with endless adoration.

_____

_____

Until the Day Dawns

June 25, 2012

And so we have the prophetic word confirmed, which you do well to heed as a light that shines in a dark place, until the day dawns and the morning star rises in your hearts... - 2 Peter 1:19.

Webster's Dictionary defines prophecy as "a declaration of something to come," so when God speaks to me about my future, I consider His words to be prophecy. Whether it's personal prophecy or a major prophecy from the Bible, we are told to heed the prophetic word as "a light that shines in a dark place..." Yes, the promises of God help to steer us through the darkest stormy nights. When all seems lost, these words from Him are a sure and steady guide, leading us always to the dawn.

A few days ago, the Spirit spoke to me regarding the years ahead. He sweetly said, *"Don't worry about your future. Jesus has already gone ahead and set it right for You."* Oh, such beautiful words! They tell me that my future is good. Since Jesus has "gone ahead," then all is certainly well, and it's filled with God's purpose for me! Answered prayer awaits me there!

With every dawn comes light, warmth and vision. But one aspect of dawn that is often overlooked is the "morning star." This star in the eastern sky is actually the planet, Venus—perfectly positioned to reflect the sun just before it rises. The morning star of scripture refers to Jesus. For people of faith, His presence during the night is assurance of good things to come. Still unseen but certainly on the way, each blessing is scheduled to appear at a predetermined dawn. Just as He has ordered the sun to rise for us each day, He has set into motion the answers to our prayers (John 4:13,14).

If we take heed to God's word in the dark of night, then the Morning Star will certainly rise in our hearts. The embers of struggling faith will be stirred into a powerful, blazing fire. Revived and fully awake, we will work and pray and bring God's Kingdom from Heaven to Earth.

Thank You, Lord, for going before us to fill our future with beauty and purpose. Thank You for paving the roads ahead with goodness and mercy. Help us to keep our eyes firmly fixed on You, our bright Morning Star, as You remind us of the glorious dawn that is coming. Let our words and prayers always reflect this expectation.

_____

_____

_____

_____

_____

_____

_____

_____

_____

_____

_____

_____

_____

_____

_____

_____

Standing on Truth

October 14, 2006

God spoke to me in a dream last week. He told me to "stand" on everything that He's taught me so far. I know that sounds quite simple, and it's something we all should remember to do. But the enemy is skilled at distracting us from the basics of Christianity.

In my dream, I was fleeing from enemy soldiers who planned to kill me. I was hiding out in a dark, abandoned room. Near the top of one wall was a small window, and right beneath it was a very tall chest of drawers. By standing on top of this towering piece of furniture, I was able to escape through the window to freedom in the countryside.

While I was interpreting the dream, God pointed out that a chest of drawers is a storage place for personal possessions. Then He explained that the contents of the drawers are spiritual treasures that I have gathered over the years. I must climb to the top and stand on them. I must use them to outwit the enemy.

Through other elements of the dream, God showed me that I sometimes lapse into fighting battles in my own strength and reasoning. Instead, I must use the mighty spiritual weapons that He's given to me. *Nothing else will work.*

The enemy tempts us to react with human effort, but this trap of futility will drain our energy. If we persist in our efforts, they will slowly destroy our hope by causing repeated failure. We must stop to consider the weapons in our God-given arsenals, then stand on these valuable truths. They will expose and disarm the enemy, giving us victory in every battle.

We must ignore the frightful noise of this world and turn our ears to the voice of God.

Trust in the Lord with all your heart, and lean not on your own understanding; in all your ways acknowledge Him, and He shall direct your paths - Proverbs 3:5-6.

Thank You, Lord, for every precept, every insight—every weapon of warfare that You've helped us stash away in our hearts. Please give us the strength and wisdom we need to use these treasures well.

_____

_____

_____

_____

_____

_____

_____

_____

_____

_____

_____

_____

_____

_____

_____

_____

_____

_____

Dry Spells

May 18, 2009

When I don't receive a personal word from God in the space of a week, then I consider myself to be in a dry spell. This happened to me a few weeks ago. I hadn't heard from the Lord in a while, and now some situations were "heating up." I wanted direction and encouragement from God, but this simply wasn't happening. As a result, I handled my problems according to principle. I relied on wisdom from the Bible and God's personal words to me in the past. I knew He was near, and I refused to overreact just because I didn't hear His voice. God doesn't pout, so there had to be a good reason for His silence.

In case the problem was with me, I did a personal inventory and confessed some wrong attitudes and behaviors. I admitted my nonchalance about a particular matter and asked God to change my heart. Now, with all this checked off my list, I turned the situation completely over to the Lord. I wasn't very happy, but I stayed in the Word, continued to pray, and trusted that "all was well." I didn't know what else to do.

Another couple of days went by, when I found myself thinking of the words "dry spell." Then I was reminded of a personal prophecy that I received years ago: God told me that I was like a tree, and He was causing my roots to grow very deep. After these thoughts came another reminder—that during dry spells, the roots of a tree will reach more deeply for water. *Ahhh! How very sweet to hear God's voice and His explanation for being silent. He was causing my roots to r-e-a-c-h.*

For he shall be like a tree planted by the waters, which spreads out its roots by the river, and will not fear when heat comes; but its leaf will be green, and will not be anxious in the year of drought, nor will cease from yielding fruit - Jeremiah 17:8.

How thirsty are you for the "Fountain of Living Waters"? When the droughts come and the River appears to dry up, will your roots reach deep in search of Him? How desperately will you seek those aquifers and bubbling springs that you cannot live without?

Thank You, Lord, for creating us with a strong thirst for You. We can't go too far or do very much without needing a deep drink of Your living water. Even sleeping makes us thirsty for time alone with You.

_____

_____

_____

_____

_____

_____

_____

_____

_____

_____

_____

_____

_____

_____

_____

_____

_____

_____

Disabling the Enemy

August 5, 2008

Every day should include some focused spiritual warfare—to protect what is ours and to take new ground. Because God intends for us to be victorious, He's given us powerful weapons to use against the demonic realm. Right now, I want to talk about the weapon of praise—a Christian's nuclear warhead.

A few days ago, I was spending time alone with God. I began with individually praising the Father, Jesus and the Holy Spirit for about ten minutes. I sang praise to them for their attributes and for what they've done for me and others. Then I knelt down, closed my eyes and asked God if He had anything to tell me. Here is how He responded:

> In my mind's eye, I began seeing the face of a wild brown rabbit. Its eyes were either closed or nonexistent. Then I noticed that the top of the rabbit's head was missing. Its skull was open. The rabbit's head contained dark brown, crumbly, decaying material. This was an ugly picture. I didn't know what it meant, and I didn't want to look at it. I asked God to erase this if it wasn't from Him, but He didn't remove it. The picture remained in my mind.

I felt compelled to learn what the rabbit symbolized, so I went to the internet and to my books about dreams and visions. Two sources told me that a rabbit is an unclean animal that represents Satan or evil spirits. Another source said that rabbits symbolize "rapid multiplication," but I ruled that out for this context. Equipped with the knowledge that rabbits symbolize impurity and evil, I began praying about the vision. God soon revealed its meaning:

> The vision was a picture of what happens to the enemy when God is praised. When I worship God, as I had just finished doing before I received the vision, then demons are immobilized. The enemy's mind becomes rotting waste, and its eyes become blind.

How can evil prevail if it cannot think or see?

This message is for all of us. We're to move ahead in God's purpose with praise on our lips, destroying the enemy as we go. No matter how we feel—whether tired, afraid, discouraged or disgusted by this world—we must always praise the Lord. Don't forget that Jesus' blood was spilled to pay for each victory. The battles are already won. We're simply collecting the spoils!

Yours, O Lord, is the greatness, the power and the glory, the victory and the majesty; for all that is in Heaven and in Earth is Yours; Yours is the kingdom, O Lord, and You are exalted as head over all. Both riches and honor come from You, and You reign over all. In Your hand is power and might; in Your hand it is to make great and to give strength to all. Now therefore, our God, we thank You and praise Your glorious name – 1 Chronicles 29:11-13.

We praise You, Lord, this very minute! Your love lifts us high! Your wisdom guides us through the day with significant purpose! Your strength keeps us from falling! Your creation delights our senses! And this is only a foretaste of eternity with You!

_____

_____

_____

_____

_____

_____

_____

_____

_____

_____

_____

Wake Up!

September 10, 2006

Every morning of my recent vacation, I woke to the bold, shrill call of an Osprey that perched in a towering palm tree across the road. The first time this happened I thought of how the bird was acting just like a rooster, announcing the start of a fresh new day. Then I began thinking of how the church needs to be more spiritually alert and that God is sending wake-up calls. I wrote this down so I wouldn't forget. *This could be a good article.*

A few days later I picked up my notes, but they didn't make much sense. I wondered why I thought an Osprey's loud morning voice could offer a lesson for the church. *How did I come up with that? I must be careful with what I write.* Then God spoke to me. He explained that my scribbled memo didn't come through human reasoning. *"I'm the One who inspired those thoughts,"* He said. I was then reminded that I've been given the gift of prophecy for a purpose. The simple message I had received must be delivered:

God says, *"Wake up, church!"*

There. I've delivered the message. Now, how will you respond? What is God asking of you personally that is sleepily pushed aside, day after day? The time has come to do it!

Is God calling you to spend more time in prayer? *Do it now!*

Should you be reading more of the Word? *Do it now!*

Has God asked you to humble yourself in a situation? *Do it now!*

Has God convicted you of a sin? Then repent! *Do it now!*

Is God telling you to help someone? *Do it now!*

Lethargy can be deadly, so shake it off! Take that first step of obedience. Then take another. Every time you obey the Lord, your spirit becomes more aligned with Him and increasingly more alert. Before you know it, you're wide awake and helping others to "rise and shine."

Awake, awake! Put on your strength, O Zion; put on your beautiful garments, O Jerusalem, the holy city! For the uncircumcised and the unclean shall no longer come to you. Shake yourself from the dust, arise; sit down, O Jerusalem! Loose yourself from the bonds of your neck, O captive daughter of Zion! - Isaiah 52:1-2.

We will rise early in the morning, Lord, to spend more time with You. In Your presence we'll find strength and direction for the day ahead. We'll find reason to stay awake.

_____

_____

_____

_____

_____

_____

_____

_____

_____

_____

_____

_____

_____

_____

_____

When God Repeats Himself

November 12, 2015

Over the years, I've learned that if God repeats Himself, then I should pay extra close attention. Currently, I'm *riveted* to what He's saying. Once or twice a day for a couple of weeks, the Lord has reminded me that "all things are new." I've responded to Him with praise and prayer and spiritual warfare. In my zeal to spread this good news, I've written a short blog post on the subject and also an article that's focused on the following words from Isaiah:

Behold, I am doing a new thing; now it springs forth, do you not perceive it? - Isaiah 43:19 ESV.

This morning, the subject came up again with new intensity: I sat in my rocking chair, hoping to connect with God in a tranquil, early-morning way. (Isn't this how Jesus did it—sitting on a comfortable rock, listening to the birds, and watching the dawn unfold as He quietly talked with His Father?) But I was having trouble being "tranquil." My mind was here and there and everywhere. I apologized to God a few times, then tried to focus on His presence—to no avail.

Finally, I stood up and began to praise the Lord. I boldly declared His worthiness to be praised, and I spoke of His accomplishments in my heart and elsewhere in my life. I praised Him for His work of making all things new. And *that* was when a floodgate opened on the theme of "all things being new." The Holy Spirit started giving me words to proclaim, pausing only long enough to let me write them down because of their importance. I'll share with you my notes because someone may be helped by them:

- All things are NEW! Today, nothing submits to demonic control or bows to anger and unforgiveness. Things are not the way they've always been.

- All things are NEW, according to the will of God—aligning with the heart and mind of God—concurring with the written word of God—agreeing with all that proceeds from the mouth of God, in whatever voice He uses!

- These things shall BE! These things ARE!

- Today is a NEW DAY! Let the Word of the Lord go forth upon the Earth and not return void!!!

Therefore, if anyone is in Christ, he is a new creation; old things have passed away; behold, all things have become new – 2 Corinthians 5:17.

After this interaction with God, I was fully awake. Any chance for tranquility was gone. Could it be that Jesus was not tranquil either when meeting His Father on the mountain at dawn? Could it be that His joy could not be contained in quietness? Maybe Jesus danced and sang with the birds and the rising sun. Maybe He was excited about His Father's love and the glory soon to come. Jesus certainly knew that His imminent death and resurrection would change everything. Surely, He was thrilled about rescuing humanity from the terrible death-grip of sin.

I hope that *you* will join in Jesus' excitement by declaring each day that things have changed. Whatever needs fixing, according to the Father's will, let's believe and declare that it is absolutely, irreversibly NEW!

So Jesus answered and said to them, "Have faith in God. For assuredly, I say to you, whoever says to this mountain, 'Be removed and be cast into the sea,' and does not doubt in his heart, but believes that those things he says will be done, he will have whatever he says..." - Mark 11:22-23.

Dear Lord, we thank You for the power You place in the words we speak—power that will cast mountains into the sea. Thank You for the persistent reminders that all things are new. We can proclaim this truth to the weary world and watch it spring to life.

_____

_____

Joyful Expectation

May 9, 2015

For the vision is yet for the appointed time; it hastens toward the goal and it will not fail. Though it tarries, wait for it; for it will certainly come, it will not delay – Habakkuk 2:3 NASB.

Christians who hear the voice of God are anticipating much good in the days and years ahead. Why? Because the Lord has been making incredible promises to His family. Believers know that He keeps His word—and we are excited! We know the Lord has not abandoned us to terrorism and fear. His faithfulness has not ended.

You may be wondering, "What about the Christians in Europe who were publicly executed because of their faith?" I believe those courageous saints (and others like them) were destined to make a global presentation of their love for Jesus. Their deaths were not in vain. The non-Christian world has clearly seen their willingness to die instead of renouncing the Lord. For each who gave their life, more are being eternally saved because of their bravery, including beloved family members.

But most of us will not be martyrs. We're called to "the fellowship of Jesus' sufferings" as part of our transformation process (Philippians 3:10), but probably not to the point of death. Significantly, amidst the trouble of this world, we're called to believe in the constant goodness of our Lord. We're called to embrace His amazing love—for us and for all of humanity. We're called to pray that brutality and murder will end.

As kings and priests (Revelation 5:10), Christians are bidden to pray God's will into being. The Spirit reveals the Father's plans to us, and then we intercede. We can expect to watch the mighty hands of God as they topple mountains of evil—all in answer to our prayer! So much good is happening today, all over the world. We just don't see it on the secular news.

On a personal level, I challenge you to focus on hearing the voice of God. He's waiting to talk with you about your future. Draw near to Him, and receive His vision for your destiny and for living supernaturally. I dare you to believe every word, and respond to it in faith. I invite you to walk in God's glory.

Vision and direction from the Lord is followed by a great hope of glory. *Listen!* God's voice leaps from the pages of your Bible, arrives in your dreams, and is whispered by the Spirit within you.

Your ears shall hear a word behind you, saying, "This is the way, walk in it..." – Isaiah 30:21.

Call to Me, and I will answer you, and show you great and mighty things, which you do not know – Jeremiah 33:3.

If any of you lacks wisdom, let him ask of God, who gives to all liberally and without reproach, and it will be given to him – James 1:5-7.

Thank You for Your glorious word, dear Lord. Thank You for entering our dreams and for sending us visions. Thank You for the many unique ways you speak to us each day. Thank You for calling us to walk in vibrant faith and joyful expectation of Your goodness.

_____ ____

_____

_____

_____

_____

_____

_____

_____

_____

_____

Our God of Abundance

September 7, 2016

Between the ages of eight and sixteen years old, I lived in Fort Myers, Florida. This was back in the days when life in the Sunshine State was slower and quite a bit sweeter. Now I live in central Georgia, and my yearly vacation is spent on Sanibel Island, right off the coast of Fort Myers. I'm drawn to the amazing natural beauty of the area. Sanibel is connected to the mainland by a modern causeway, but when I was a child, we could only reach it by ferry.

Ibis, Egrets, and Herons are an elegant but common sight on the shores of Sanibel. They're joined by multitudes of Seagulls, Terns, Skimmers, Willets, Plovers, and so many more, including the humans who walk among them. If you know where to look, the large Roseate Spoonbills are easy to find. Eagles, Osprey, and Pelicans patrol every shore and skillfully capture fish by zooming down from above. For eyes that crave botanical adventure, a variety of palms and lush subtropical flora are pure delight. Exotic plants and blooms are conventional fare on this island. Lizards scamper everywhere. The sound of frogs invades the night, and hundreds of sea turtles hatch annually from these protected shores. Even with all of this to offer, Sanibel's main draw is the vast array of beautiful shells that are heaped onto the beach with each incoming tide. The island is positioned and shaped in such a way that it captures a lion's share of this natural bounty.

Do my words sound like a promotion of Sanibel Island? I suppose they do, but my underlying purpose is to present an aspect of God, so I will continue—with much enthusiasm.

The timeshare week that I own on Sanibel is always at the end of August, in prime hurricane season. "Week 35" is usually bright, with only some typical afternoon thunder storms. I have, however, encountered the fury of hurricanes from the safe perspective of a gulf-front condominium. I've also walked on hurricane-battered shores, amidst the salty wind and spray. To experience this power firsthand is awe-inspiring. In 2002, I watched Hurricane Gustav speed by, keeping a respectful distance while putting on a blustery show. Just three years later, deadly Katrina thundered around the tip of Florida, right in front of my eyes—raging at category five.

I've just returned from my 2016 vacation on Sanibel Island, and I am calling it "Hurricane Hermine week." For three days, the gulf water was bright and calm. But as Hermine made her entrance, she slowly gathered strength, and things began to change. Sanibel shores are not known for their surf, but hurricanes bring larger waves, and along with them comes the bonus of extra shells. *Lots* of extra shells.

On my last day of vacation, I said to the Lord, *"I'm going down to the beach to gather shells. Please talk with me while I'm there."*

As soon as I opened the front door, I heard the sound of crashing waves. Following a boardwalk through the natural area, I could see storm-tossed water ahead, but I was mostly impressed with the intense sound. Then God announced to me, *"I Am ROARING!"* He wanted me to know that the "voice of the surf" was His own:

The voice of the Lord is over the waters; the God of glory thunders; the Lord is over many waters. The voice of the Lord is powerful; the voice of the Lord is full of majesty – Psalm 29:3-4.

God revealed that the time for change has come—that He is moving—that He is roaring with purpose and imminent manifest power. I thanked Him for the encouragement, but He wasn't finished speaking. A few minutes later, as I began to get enthused about the increased amount and variety of shells, I heard Him say, *"As you can see, I Am a God of abundance. My heart is one of abundance. I long to pour treasure upon My people. Those who are prepared and expecting My blessing will receive great riches in all areas of life—in addition to the financial realm."* God explained that storms are often His vehicle of provision. And for those who have leaned on Him wholeheartedly during these storms, His profusion of gifts will soon be on shore.

Dearest El Shaddai, our all-sufficient God; You are the One who supplies what we need—not just barely, but according to Your riches in glory. Thank You for revealing Your desire to lavish us with treasure. Thank You for the storms that position us perfectly to receive Your wealth.

A Monumental Display

March 18, 2007

I've been thinking about the realities of hell. A few days ago, I read a detailed description of this horrific place, written by a man who claims to have been there for twenty-three minutes (23 Minutes in Hell, by Bill Wiese). Images of terror, torture and misery are now imprinted in my memory. While considering the torments of hell, I began thinking of all the people who don't know God. Then the Holy Spirit reminded me of the following verse from Romans that speaks of personal accountability:

For ever since the world was created, people have seen the earth and sky. Through everything God made, they can clearly see His invisible qualities—His eternal power and divine nature. So they have no excuse for not knowing God - Romans 1:20 NLT.

I explained to God that I was mostly concerned for the people who are deceived. I was worried about the ones who would respond to those "invisible qualities" presented by His creation—*IF* they weren't blinded and confused by the evil influence around them.

Then the revelation came! Christians must *pray* for God to reveal Himself to such a degree that blind eyes will open wide. We must pray for a monumental display of God's truth and power that will remove every trace of deception.

To save His people in the past, God has parted the sea, stopped the flow of a river, and even made the sun stand still for twenty-four hours. I believe He is ready to reveal Himself again in supernatural ways—to the largest population ever. Let's pray that God will exhibit His glory to a magnitude that exposes all deceit. When this occurs, people will be more accountable than ever before. Their decisions to embrace or reject our Lord will be made after knowing His truth.

Dear Lord, please remove all apathy about the reality of hell. Open our eyes so we will pray for the vision of others. Let Your beautiful, saving truth be fully released throughout the earth. Let the light of Your glory shine.

ENCOUNTERING GOD EACH DAY

The Gift of Life

December 12, 2009

In Him was life, and the life was the light of men - John 1:4.

Over 2000 years ago, our Heavenly Father sent the gift of Life to Earth. The gift was delivered to a stable in the form of a holy newborn child. As the angels first beheld the infant Son of God, they were surely in awe of the perfect Life before their eyes.

I once had the privilege of watching a human birth. Upon arrival, the baby was immediately placed on a table to be closely examined by nurses. I remember the surprising glow of purity coming from the small pink body. I realized the child was still untouched by sin and would be like this for a very short while.

Jesus also arrived untouched by sin, but He remained that way. His purity made an impact wherever He went. The world reacted to Jesus' lack of sin by mistreating Him, but He always responded with holiness, love, and precious truth. Jesus stayed in close contact with the Father, and He never forgot His mission. Not once was He distracted by this world or pulled off course.

Christians quickly learn that the gift of Life overflows with love and power—all for us to use and share with others. Mercy has thawed our cold hearts, so we can forgive. We love the unlovely because Jesus does it through us. And once we're in this loving mode, we joyfully teach, encourage, heal, deliver, and a whole lot more. Our prayers are born of the Spirit, and they rise on wings of faith. The beautiful Life within us is boundless.

Both enlightened and empowered, we are now truly alive! Holding the hand of God, we step into our destiny—bringing goodness and change to our needy world.

Thank You, Father, for Your gift of Life. Jesus is completely "above and beyond"—always saving, healing, and giving. He is everything we need.

We Are Never Alone

September 29, 2007

The Lord is with us at all times, whether we're aware of it or not. Awake or asleep, in the Spirit or in the flesh, Christians are never alone. When we first wake in the morning, if we focus on the presence of God, we'll soon feel His comforting love.

If the enemy dares to launch a pre-dawn attack, we can quickly convert each anxious thought to a prayer for help—never to an unknown, far-away God, but to the One who lives within us. On mornings that start out peacefully (as well as those that don't), we can praise the Lord, soak up His love, and ask for direction with matters that lie ahead. We may hear His answers right away or sprinkled throughout the day.

On whatever note the day begins, connecting with God is the best way to proceed. Including Him in our thoughts from morning 'til night will guarantee good results.

I have set the Lord always before me; because He is at my right hand I shall not be moved – Psalm 16:8.

Dear sweet Lord, we love Your abiding presence. You bring stability and truth to every hour of the day. Your wisdom whispers at every turn, and Your mercy is close at hand. We are blessed and honored by your company.

_____

_____

_____

_____

_____

_____

_____

The Road That Jesus Walks

February 24, 2006

New Christians are met with wave after wave of refreshing life-changing truth. This includes healing truth, nurturing truth—whatever truth is needed most. Our Father loves to build us up. But after a while, when He knows that we're ready, the truth will come in less appealing forms. It won't always sound as nice or taste as sweet as when we first began.

Truth will either tear us down or strengthen us—whichever the Spirit intends. Our selfish inclinations have to go, and truth will strip them away. But truth will also fill us with more of our holy God.

In theory, the process of cleansing, growth and total submission to God sounds quite simple—also noble and exciting. But in reality, letting go of our sinful, independent nature is difficult and painful. If there were an alternate route, not many would travel this bumpy, distressing road.

I've heard it said that God is much more concerned with our sanctification than He is with our contentment. I know this is true because my "comfort zone" disappeared over 20 years ago. My personal road to humility and holiness has been watered with tears and lined with the marks of my dragging feet.

Though I sometimes slow down, I will never leave the path that God has set before me. Yes, I could choose another direction, but I'm always compelled to stay on this course. *Why?* Because this is the road that Jesus walks. He is the One who's captured my heart.

Who may ascend into the hill of the Lord? Or who may stand in His holy place? He who has clean hands and a pure heart, who has not lifted up his soul to an idol, nor sworn deceitfully. He shall receive blessing from the Lord, and righteousness from the God of his salvation – Psalm 24:3-5.

Dear Lord, please keep us always on roads that You have designed. Some will be high with beautiful views, and others will wind through deep and frightful valleys. But each road is good that keeps us walking by Your side, leaning entirely on You for what we need.

The Way

November 19, 2007

Years ago, God gave me a vision regarding my future. This preview has served as a guide to keep me moving in the right direction. When God first gave me a glimpse of the road ahead, I was very excited. I began work on primary tasks with energy and passion. I would do a *great* job. God would be pleased with my effort—I was certain of that. *And then the enlightenment began.*

With the passing of time, I've discovered that beyond a doubt, I am weak and inept. I can do nothing great. Not without God, that is. (Though painful to accept, this humbling awareness is critical for success in the kingdom of God.) In the wake of my new self-assessment came an admonition regarding heavy dependence on people, systems or things: The Lord will not allow it.

My path continues to narrow, but that's okay. Every step brings me to a deeper understanding that Jesus truly is "the Way." He leads me through the tangles and trials of each new day—all the while teaching, protecting and providing for me. He keeps me forever inspired by His brilliant presence and powerful words.

Thus says the Lord, your Redeemer, the Holy One of Israel: "I am the Lord your God, who teaches you to profit, who leads you by the way you should go - Isaiah 48:17.

Thank You, Lord, for personal revelation. Providing us with vision for the days and years ahead is a reflection of Your fierce desire to lead us forward, always toward You. We thank You also for the narrow road that allows little room for distraction.

The Fellowship of His Suffering

April 10, 2009

With the Christian life comes a certain amount of suffering. We are set apart—often afflicted but always comforted. When our hearts are submitted to God, then sorrow brings us into closer fellowship with Him—into a place where we count it an honor to feel the sting of rejection or the pain of ill-treatment.

...that I may know Him and the power of His resurrection, and the fellowship of His sufferings... - Philippians 3:10.

Thank You, Lord, for putting us in hostile places where finding the peace of Your presence is paramount. We're blessed to follow in Your shoes. Thank You for those alarming situations that teach us not to fear—for those dark paths and valleys where we learn first-hand that every "giant" has been already slain by You.

Thank You, Lord, that when we're despised by the world for being "foolish and weak," we are actually flying high, soaring on Your triumphant wings of truth. Thank You for making us a threat to the enemy—so much that we're under attack. Thank You for the victory that is always ours to take.

Thank You, Lord, for "the joy that is set before us" as we take up our crosses daily, releasing Your resurrection power into the world.

For our light affliction, which is but for a moment, is working for us a far more exceeding and eternal weight of glory... - 2 Corinthians 4:17.

We anticipate Your splendor, Lord, unfolding throughout eternity. All tears will be forgotten—all pain and sorrow left behind. We see that even now, upon this fallen Earth, Your glory reaches into the darkness, gathering those You love.

_____

_____

_____

The Breath of God

September 28, 2013

And the LORD God formed man of the dust of the ground, and breathed into his nostrils the breath of life; and man became a living being – Genesis 2:6-7.

At the beginning of creation, after God had sculpted Adam, His powerful breath filled this man with life. Today, this same breath keeps each of *us* alive. And if we choose, it will keep us in the center of God's will.

And when He had said this, He breathed on them, and said to them, "Receive the Holy Spirit..." - John 20:22.

Much comes forth when God exhales, in both His speaking and His quietness. When we draw near to the Lord, His breath surrounds and infuses our being. It keeps darkness at a distance, and it creates the perfect environment for all that is good.

In my quiet time with the Lord, when I'm keenly aware of His nearness and His "breathing," my spirit is filled with peace. I know that all is well. I'm sure that everything I've struggled with and prayed over is being held in God's hands, enclosed in His love.

Be still, and know that I am God... – Psalm 46:10.

It's important that believers take time to "be still" and enjoy the presence of God. This Life in our innermost being is the source of all that we're destined to be.

Thank You, Lord, for choosing to live in the depths of every Christian. Your breath and Your heartbeat give us life that is truly worth living.

_____

_____

_____

_____

_____

Enter His Rest

July 8, 2008

Human beings—body, mind and spirit—need plenty of rest from our labors. God chose to rest after His work of creation, and we should follow His example.

And on the seventh day God ended His work which He had done, and He rested on the seventh day from all His work which He had done - Genesis 2:2.

We all know how to rest when we've finished working. But the Lord wants us to be at rest *during* our work and during the many hardships we face. As we turn to God for support with daily challenges, He is glad to get involved. When we ask Him for help with the raging storms of life, we see Him calm our troubled waters. Through this experience with God, we learn how to be at peace in a variety of situations. Each involvement of the Lord on our behalf becomes a stepping stone for entering more deeply into His rest. At every step, we learn to trust Him with more of what we hold dear.

"Trust in God" is the name of this precious key that opens the door to His rest. "Have Faith in God" could also be engraved on the key, since trust and faith are synonymous. Whatever we choose to call it, the key should be used at every opportunity. Sadly, many Christians turn to deceptive remedies of this world instead of using the key that comes from our Creator. Let us beware of settling for any type of sedation or distraction. These will never supply the perfect rest that only comes from trusting the Lord.

Therefore, since a promise remains of entering His rest, let us fear lest any of you seem to have come short of it - Hebrews 4:1.

Trust in You, Lord, always brings the sweetest rest. Once we have a taste of this, we cannot settle for anything less. Rest brings strength to reach for more of Your truth—for the peace, hope, and renewal that is only found in You.

The Fullness of God

November 29, 2008

For this reason I bow my knees to the Father of our Lord Jesus Christ...that you, being rooted and grounded in love, may be able to comprehend with all the saints what is the width and length and depth and height—to know the love of Christ which passes knowledge; that you may be filled with all the fullness of God - Ephesians 3:14, 17-19.

The "fullness of God" is a gift that waits to be valued and claimed. Nominal Christians don't take the offer seriously. They're blinded to the potential of this phenomenal gift and the responsibility they have to receive it. Their lifeless "religion" has replaced God's truth and power. Those who trifle with God may have fleeting moments of spiritual connection, but they generally operate by human reasoning. Instead of being dependent on God, they lean on their own understanding.

If, perhaps, I've just described you, then please consider what would transpire if you seek the Lord with energy and passion—first submitting your life to Him, then obeying every prompting of His Spirit. Before long, your spiritual hearing would be perfectly tuned to God's frequency. As a beloved friend of God, your life would be a vessel of His healing, transforming power. This power would flow through your words and your touch. Even your shadow could make a difference. God's fullness in you would set many captives free.

Most assuredly, I say to you, he who believes in Me, the works that I do he will do also; and greater works than these he will do, because I go to My Father - John 14:12.

Jesus tells us we'll do *greater* works than He did while on Earth. He expects miracles to be a routine part of our day. We should not be ensnared by religious facade or lack of faith when we're free to believe God's mighty Word. If we follow the voice of the Spirit, always trusting and obeying, the Lord will respond by giving us more of Himself. One day we'll be completely filled with love and life and power. We'll be filled with all that God is.

Please remove all blindness, Lord. Remove every scale from our eyes and any cotton from our ears. Please wash away all pretense. We want our hearts set afire by Your Spirit. We want to believe You to the uttermost. Help us to pursue You and overtake You, as much as You will allow.

_____

_____

_____

_____

_____

_____

_____

_____

_____

_____

_____

_____

_____

_____

_____

_____

_____

_____

Choose Joy

April 9, 2010

Friends and family are a blessing, but they can sometimes bring us pain. Harsh words and selfish behavior may hit us hard if we're standing in the line of fire. Being hurt by others is part of the human experience, but whether we're victimized or victorious is always our choice.

Recently, after going through some painful events, I was trying to get them into perspective. A few things were already clear to me: I would not give up on the people involved, and I refused to wallow in self-pity. I wanted restoration for everyone concerned.

I asked the Lord to ease my pain, heal my wounds, and help the situation. Before long, He spoke two powerful words of life to me: *"Choose joy."*

Yes, of course! The joy of the Lord is our strength! Just a few weeks earlier, God had blessed me with a heavy dose of His joy, and the experience was still fresh in my mind. I knew this divine energy was exactly what I needed. The Spirit was reminding me to look at the beauty of God instead of the troubling event.

You have made known to me the ways of life; You will make me full of joy in Your presence - Acts 2:28.

I believe that choosing joy is literally choosing the presence of God. This simple act of faith will move His heart to bless and transform us, along with those we love.

We choose You, Lord. We choose Your kindness and Your love. We choose Your strong desire to transform our families and inhabit our relationships. We choose to embrace the joy that is always found in You.

Seated in the Heavenlies

April 19, 2006

Today's sun had not yet risen when I was given this reminder: *"You are seated in the heavenlies with Christ."*

What a wonderful truth to begin my day! Because I am in the heavenlies with Christ, then all things—including all of my problems—are under His feet and also under mine.

And He put all things under His feet, and gave Him to be head over all things to the church, which is His body, the fullness of Him who fills all in all - Ephesians 1:22-23.

Since I abide in Christ, I sit in the same heavenly seat that He does, right beside the Father. When I'm submitted to Jesus' headship, I have authority and power. Instead of fretting about the obstacles before me or the problems of this world, I will boldly proclaim scripture and know that it will come to pass. Because Jesus intercedes with love, I will do the same.

Dear sweet Spirit of God, we thank You for guarding us at night and greeting us with beautiful truth in the morning. How we love Your constant attention to our lives.

Do You Really Know Him?

January 28, 2006

Going to church is a very good thing, unless it substitutes for building a real relationship with God. If church attendance and a few highly visible good works are the sum of your Christianity, then you have been deceived.

Not everyone who says to Me, 'Lord, Lord,' shall enter the kingdom of heaven, but he who does the will of My Father in heaven. Many will say to Me in that day, 'Lord, Lord, have we not prophesied in Your name, cast out demons in Your name, and done many wonders in Your name?' And then I will declare to them, 'I never knew you; depart from Me, you who practice lawlessness!' - Matthew 7:21-23.

Those who consistently do the Father's will shall enter the kingdom of Heaven. It won't be those who perform the occasional good deed when it's convenient and when it helps their image. And it won't be those who choose political correctness instead of holiness. True Christians are those who submit to God unswervingly and wholeheartedly—even when it hurts.

Doing what God requires will generate a close relationship. This intimacy in turn arouses more obedience. Both intimacy and obedience are fueled by the word of God. Because the Bible is readily available, Christians are responsible for seeking God and learning what He wants from us.

Obedience to the Father's will is not a piece of cake. It can't be effectively accomplished without abiding in Christ (John 15:4). While walking with the Lord, learning humility, and how to partake of His grace, we gradually get to know Him. Our desire to fully obey Him will grow each day under His tender loving care.

> **You are My friends if you do whatever I command you - John 15:14.**

If your Sunday morning Christianity is only a hollow pretense, then you're literally playing with fire. Please spend time with God before it's too late. Learn what He requires of you. And by all means, take His hand and hold on tight. You were not created to be apart.

Knowing You, Lord, is the greatest blessing given to man. Please hold us close. Keep us always aware of our need for You. Open our hearts to receive more and more of Your love.

Value Beyond Measure

September 6, 2014

O LORD God of hosts, who is mighty as you are, O LORD, with your faithfulness all around you? – Psalm 89:8 ESV.

The value of God's faithfulness is completely beyond measure. Apart from this aspect of His character, our Christian faith would have nothing to support it. Hope could not exist.

Holy scripture is our written guide for living, but it's also the plumb line that reveals God's perfect record of keeping His word. Our Helper, the Holy Spirit, reminds us what God has said so we can navigate into the future with a strong and vibrant faith.

God's word is His holy covenant with "all who love Him and keep His commandments" (Deuteronomy 7:9). As the Sacrificial Lamb, Jesus ensures that the covenant won't be broken by our sin.

The powers of darkness never rest from maligning the character of our Lord, so we often need reminders of relevant truth—especially about God's faithfulness. God loves to reveal Himself, so we can ask expectantly for displays of His integrity.

God's faithfulness is a thing of beauty. It can be clearly seen in the ongoing transformation of every born-again Christian. At first we are quite a mess, but God is faithful to finish what He has begun (Philippians 1:6). His dependability is seen each time the sun rises and sets, and also when the seasons change (Genesis 8:22). We see it again whenever the rain falls (Job 5:10) and when the crops are ready for harvest (Deuteronomy 11:14).

The faithful heart of God is glorious. It is worthy to be praised, even before we see Him move on our behalf. Before the prodigal child comes home, we need to cry, "Hallelujah! God will save this wayward one! (Luke 15:3-7)" Before our financial needs are met, we should thank God for His promise of provision (Malachi 3:10)! Before our destinies fully unfold, we must praise the Lord for His magnificent plans (Isaiah 60)! God's faithfulness covers every need, and it will surely endure forever (Psalm 117:2)!

Dear Lord, You are the Solid Rock who keeps us safe from shifting sands. Your stability gives us faith and hope for all good things. From the bottom of our hearts, we thank You for always keeping Your word.

_____

_____

_____

_____

_____

_____

_____

_____

_____

_____

_____

_____

_____

_____

_____

_____

_____

_____

_____

_____

His Eyes, His Ears, His Heart

April 18, 2010

To be victorious in our tribulations, we must stay focused on the Lord. The majority of battles take place in our minds, so our best defense lies in joining with God and His perspective: How does He view the situation? How does He feel about it? What does He want to do?

I've been talking with a young Christian friend whose job situation is unstable because of reduced funding. God has given her a good amount of peace, but as we talked, I realized she was too concerned about pleasing her professional peers. If she was to be laid off due to downsizing, she wanted to be remembered as "very successful" while she was there, even though she was a novice in this career field. While my friend and I were talking, the Spirit gave me His perspective, so I passed it on: *"Don't forget that God's measure of success is often entirely different than man's measure of success."* This young woman responded immediately with excitement and joy. A reminder that God's opinion is the one that matters had quickly set her on higher, happier ground. Our conversation ended with my advice to stay focused on the Lord.

Within a few days, I was able to apply the wisdom of "staying focused on God" to my own life. I found myself viewing a problem through my own understanding and therefore having strong, negative emotions. I was seeing with my own eyes and feeling with my own heart. I'm sure God was testing my willingness to set aside my intense feelings. He wanted me to consider and accept His view of the matter. I obeyed, and the Spirit quickly calmed my inner turmoil.

Obedience is always pleasing to God, and it's especially sweet to us when followed by a visible move of His hand. But this issue goes even deeper: When we obey, then *our* problems combined with *God's* solutions become doorways to a higher level of Christian life. We move beyond our routine of merely "passing tests." We step more fully into God's glorious presence.

It's true! When we consistently choose to see with God's eyes, hear with God's ears, and feel with God's heart, we are choosing to experience *Him.*

**In that day the deaf shall hear the words of the book, and the eyes of the blind shall see out of obscurity and out of darkness. The humble also shall increase their joy in the LORD, and the poor among men shall rejoice in the Holy One of Israel –
Isaiah 29:18-19.**

In Your wisdom, Lord, You have created us with desperate need for You. And in Your love, You meet us every day to resolve our needs. Our requirements vary, and so do Your solutions, but Your presence is always amazing. Experiencing You is forever reason to rejoice.

_____

_____

_____

_____

_____

_____

_____

_____

_____

_____

_____

_____

_____

_____

God Is in the Room

April 23, 2011

If we are born again, the Lord goes with us everywhere. We know His indwelling Spirit is ready to help in our many times of need. But how often do we consider the impact of this holy presence on the people around us—not through what we say or do, but simply because *God is in the room*?

Please take a minute to visualize yourself walking through a doorway with the Lord by your side. He is the Most High God—Creator of all that exists. He gleams with holiness. He radiates love. His power bursts forth in continuing flashes of light. This is not currently seen by human eyes, but even so, it is spiritual reality.

Being acutely aware of God's presence will bring us both security and humility. This also makes us responsible to "let God be God" as we move through the day.

Certainly, the Lord wants to speak and act through us—but not all the time. Being filled with the Spirit doesn't mean we should always be talking or doing good works. I think sometimes our activity disrupts what God has planned. If we get too busy "behaving like Christians," then we're less apt to hear the Spirit's guiding voice, and before long we're actually on our own. More will be accomplished when we learn the value of being quiet and still, as God requires. We can silently pray and praise the Lord, loosing His fullness into the space around us.

As Christ abides in us, His power, peace and holiness *will* escape the confines of our inner being, even with our mouths closed and our hands and feet inactive. God will not be tightly contained in anyone. As Moses returned from Mount Sinai, his followers saw that he glowed with the light of God's presence (Exodus 34:29). This may be the case with us one day. And as with Peter, the mere casting of our shadow might loose God's healing or deliverance (Acts 5:15). The Lord's light and life in us will find a way to touch the world. We can always trust the Spirit to choose how this will happen.

Be still, and know that I am God; I will be exalted among the nations, I will be exalted in the earth! - Psalm 46:10.

Thank You, Lord, for crossing every threshold with us. Please help us convey You properly to the needful ones around us. We want to see Your glory unfold in our assigned domains. Yes, Lord, let your glory fall on us and on everyone in the room!

_____

_____

_____

_____

_____

_____

_____

_____

_____

_____

_____

_____

_____

_____

_____

_____

_____

_____

Lean Upon God

May 7, 2011

Some Christians only call on the Lord in times of major crisis. Sadly, this practice leaves them vulnerable through everything else in life, and this is not what God intends. The Lord has designed all of creation to lean upon Him. Man's greatest need is to know God in a personal way. All other needs are blessings if they bring us to our knees in prayer. Jesus doesn't mind that we're weak and needy. *Our problems bring out the best in Him.*

And He said to me, "My grace is sufficient for you, for My strength is made perfect in weakness." Therefore most gladly I will rather boast in my infirmities, that the power of Christ may rest upon me. Therefore I take pleasure in infirmities, in reproaches, in needs, in persecutions, in distresses, for Christ's sake. For when I am weak, then I am strong – 2 Corinthians 12:9-10.

When we draw near, the Holy Spirit whispers secrets that aid and sustain us in difficult times. One spoken word from Him delivers the push we need to march another hundred miles. A simple vision will encourage us for weeks. Godly revelation always comes with power—like a bolt of lightning to illumine our world on dark and stormy nights.

As we lean on the Lord, we are introduced to Hope. This powerful attribute of God is an exceedingly precious gift. It comes wrapped in strong sheets of purpose and is tied with bright ribbons of joy. Along with many other gifts, this beautiful Hope is free to every child of God. Our Father wants us well-equipped.

But God has chosen the foolish things of the world to put to shame the wise, and God has chosen the weak things of the world to put to shame the things which are mighty; and the base things of the world and the things which are despised God has chosen, and the things which are not, to bring to nothing the things that are, that no flesh should glory in His presence – 1 Corinthians 1:27-29.

Let's praise the Lord for revealing His grace and glory through us—the "weak and foolish" ones who are often despised in this world. As we lean upon Him, we're lifted increasingly high.

Lord, we thank You for inviting us, the weak and the despised, to Your throne of grace—for bidding us to come boldly to You with our needs (Hebrews 4:16).

_____

_____

_____

_____

_____

_____

_____

_____

_____

_____

_____

_____

_____

_____

_____

_____

_____

_____

Power, Life, and Love

June 20, 2014

While browsing through a travel magazine, looking at destinations and amenities that most people can only dream of, I received insight from the Lord. I saw that the wealthy, in their pursuit of fulfillment, are deceived about many things. They've been misled about what a truly exalted position in life consists of, what is the finest experience to be gained, and what is the greatest possession to acquire. These people seek joy in the realm of creation instead of in the Creator.

With plenty of money, I would also be tempted to pursue those far-off pristine beaches; the ones with a backdrop of coconut palms, depths of jungle growth, and the distant chatter of tropical birds. I would seek shimmering turquoise bays, enhanced by morning mist and framed by distant mountains—and I would court similar views by moonlight. These places would be discovered from the deck of an elegant teak sailing vessel.

Yes, it's easy to get caught up in the wonder of God's creation and in His generosity. The work of His hands is glorious. But a whisper from the Lord will set these places and things in their proper position. The Spirit has shown me clearly—*Jesus is far more desirable than anything He created.* In addition to His absolute purity, His matchless beauty, and His supreme sovereignty, Jesus provides the *excitement* we crave.

Please consider these three attributes of the Lord:

POWER The power that flowed from Jesus' lips created all that we see. **In the beginning was the Word, and the Word was with God, and the Word was God. He was in the beginning with God. All things were made through Him, and without Him nothing was made that was made – John 1:1-3.** This is my Lord! I will praise Him and pursue Him. I will chase after the One who makes the clouds flash and rumble on a summer evening. I will sing to the One who makes kittens purr and oceans roar.

LIFE Life springs forth with promise and joy as it fills a child at conception, then escorts it through eternity. **For You formed my inward parts; You covered me in my mother's womb. I will praise**

You, for I am fearfully and wonderfully made... – Psalm 139:13-14. Our contemplations of Jesus should always include this rich provision.

Let's also reflect on Jesus' desire to *restore* life: **He cried with a loud voice, "Lazarus, come forth!" And he who had died came out bound hand and foot with grave clothes, and his face was wrapped with a cloth. Jesus said to them, "Loose him, and let him go" – John 11:43-44.** Oh, yes! I will praise the One who gives and restores life to those I love.

<u>LOVE</u> We all agree that love has great value. **Many waters cannot quench love, nor can the floods drown it. If a man would give for love all the wealth of his house, it would be utterly despised – Song of Solomon 8:7.** Jesus is Love Incarnate. I will follow the beat of His heart forever.

<u>Power, life, and love</u>! Jesus embodies these things completely. He *is* Power. He *is* Life. He *is* Love. Never "religious" or stuffy, Jesus is *exciting!* And He is ours to enjoy forever!

Sing to the LORD a new song, and His praise in the assembly of saints... Let the saints be joyful in glory; let them sing aloud on their beds. Let the high praises of God be in their mouth, and a two-edged sword in their hand... – Psalm 149:1, 5-6.

Thank You, Jesus, for the excitement You bring to our lives. Please continue revealing Yourself to us. Keep us awake and alive to Your powerful, glorious presence. Please draw each of us closer to You, by whatever means You choose.

_____

_____

_____

_____

_____

Time Alone With God

February 2, 2013

Are you weary from battle? Are you wounded and fearful of taking another step? Does the thought of mustering up your faith for another confrontation with evil make you want to be in bed with a blanket pulled over your head? If so, then it's time for a touch from God.

David would often meet with God in the mountains after encounters with King Saul's army. Try to imagine, during your next quiet time with the Lord, that you're resting in a mountain forest. Envision yourself sitting in the shelter of a cave. Now let your mind focus on the goodness of the Lord and all He has done for you up to this point.

At the entrance of your cave, looking out on God's creation, let Him caress you with every breeze that drifts your way. Be encouraged by the cheerful song of tiny birds. Pretend that night is falling, then relax and be glad of your shelter. Inhale the clean scent of cedar and pine that is floating in from woodland heights. Allow the Lord to touch your face and kiss your brow. Let Him wipe away every tear and every fear.

I lay down and slept; I awoke, for the Lord sustained me. I will not be afraid of ten thousands of people who have set themselves against me all around – Psalm 3:5-6.

On many occasions like this, the heart of David filled with praise. His delight in the Lord overflowed into the centuries ahead. Such was the impact of his time alone with God.

While David rested and enjoyed the presence of the Lord, the desires of His heart were being met—on a mountainside retreat, as well as in the realm where he had been fighting. While David delighted, God *acted*. Ultimately, this fugitive cave dweller was crowned as King over "all Israel and Judah."

Therefore all the elders of Israel came to the king at Hebron, and King David made a covenant with them at Hebron before the Lord. And they anointed David king over Israel. David was thirty years old when he began to reign, and he reigned forty years. In Hebron he reigned over Judah seven years and six months, and

in Jerusalem he reigned thirty-three years over all Israel and Judah – 2 Samuel 5:3-5.

As with King David, the impact of our delight in the Lord will overflow and surge ahead into eternity. Riding on this triumphant wave will be the desires of our heart—the dear ones we have prayed for, along with many more who are caught up in the holy flood.

Delight yourself in the Lord, and he will give you the desires of your heart – Psalm 37:4.

We thank You, Lord, for coming close to meet our needs. Thank You for exalting us, according to Your purpose. Thank You for Your precious Word that lifts us high and lights our way. Please keep us ever dependent upon Your Presence and Your grace. Let us forever draw near to delight in You.

_____

_____

_____

_____

_____

_____

_____

_____

_____

_____

_____

_____

_____

From Failure to Victory

October 15, 2011

Now there was a long war between the house of Saul and the house of David. But David grew stronger and stronger, and the house of Saul grew weaker and weaker – 2 Samuel 3:1.

The battles we encounter in this life can be frightening. But if we abide in Christ, every skirmish is an opportunity to learn, to grow and to glorify God. No one looks forward to trouble, but without it we would miss the joy of deliverance. We would never know the thrill of victory.

Within a spiritual war zone, even our failures can be important steps toward victory if we embrace God's mighty, redeeming grace. We can look ahead with bold determination, to meet the next challenge with the strategy of God.

No matter how painful our failure, we can refuse to let it define us. *Failure should only be a teacher.* Our Christian identity lies firmly in the realm of victory.

I was once blind-sided by harsh words from an angry, controlling woman. My response was brief but much too reactive. The attacker then reported my "verbal failure" to some people that I respected. The Spirit immediately convicted me of my sin, but this woman was bent on slandering me. Circumstances prevented me from revealing to others the proper context and setting the record straight. So then, within my mind, another conflict raged. I now felt maligned and rejected. But I knew this was a test of my faith, so I called to God—the only One who could help. His response overflowed with compassion and grace. He unfolded His battle plan, showing me exactly how to pray. Within 48 hours, the enemy's canon was backfiring into its own camp. Watching the Lord act powerfully on my behalf was *priceless*.

Have you not known? Have you not heard? The everlasting God, the LORD, the Creator of the ends of the earth, neither faints nor is weary. His understanding is unsearchable. He gives power to the weak, and to those who have no might He increases strength - Isaiah 40:28, 29.

Looking humbly and unreservedly to God in the midst of weakness will always tip the scale in our favor. When His truth and revelation arrive on the scene, our prior failure becomes a monumental turning point.

Dear Lord, we thank You for going into battle with us. Under Your command, we grow wiser and stronger each day. Please teach us with every failure, and inspire us with every inch of ground that is gained.

_____

_____

_____

_____

_____

_____

_____

_____

_____

_____

_____

_____

_____

_____

_____

_____

Morning

March 4, 2006

Potential and promise arrive with the first light of dawn. Hope is infused in the morning mist to nurture our minds and spirits. Natural elements greet our senses and beckon our spirits to rejoice.

Arise, shine; for your light has come! And the glory of the Lord is risen upon you. For behold, the darkness shall cover the earth, and deep darkness the people; but the Lord will arise over you, and His glory will be seen upon you. The Gentiles shall come to your light, and kings to the brightness of your rising – Isaiah 60:1-3.

Morning is an excellent time to experience God! Step into His presence early with words of thanksgiving and praise. Draw close, and hear the beat of Love within His holy heart. Trust Him. Believe His word. Submit to His will for today. Embrace His favor and blessing.

Receive the light of God's glory that is risen upon you!

Dear sweet Jesus, we thank You for waking us this morning. We thank You for the gift of a new day that is bursting with promise and sparkling with hope.

_____

_____

_____

_____

_____

_____

_____

_____

El Shaddai

September 1, 2007

But without faith it is impossible to please Him, for he who comes to God must believe that He is, and that He is a rewarder of those who diligently seek Him - Romans 11:6.

"Shad," from God's name of El Shaddai, means "breast." For His hungry, growing children, this Breast supplies only what is good. God never gives us soda or chocolate milk, but only the purest provision that perfectly meets our needs and prepares us for the future. Because of this, we should always run to the Lord instead of turning to other sources. Our provider who owns "the cattle on a thousand hills" (Psalm 50:10) wishes to care for us well.

Yes, it's okay to seek God's hand—the provision of El Shaddai. In fact it's a privilege we should not neglect. We humans have requirements that only our God can meet. Seeking Him as our source of supply reveals our faith, and He's always pleased by that.

When we go to God for help, we come in contact with who He is. We see glimpses of His character that only a person in need can fully appreciate. And now we have a choice. We can continue to seek God's hand alone, or we can seek His hand as well as His amazing heart.

> When we boldly approach the throne of grace, our desires are purified. Our hunger to serve God and to meet *His* needs will steadily increase.

David, the shepherd who would be king, was a man with desperate needs. He often sought God's protection from those who wanted him dead. For years, he lived in mountain caves with his ragged army of men, seeking God's hand for food, water, clothing and guidance. The Lord met David's need and thereby drew him close. As a result, David became "a man after God's own heart" (Acts 13:22), unashamed of his outspoken love for the Lord.

El Shaddai, Almighty God, we thank You for Your tender care and generous provision. In the midst of nurturing and bounty, we behold the love in Your eyes, and by it we're transformed.

Let There Be Light!

January 14, 2015

Then God said, "Let there be light"—and there was light. And God saw the light, that it was good; and God divided the light from the darkness – Genesis 1:3-4.

When God created the physical world, He gave light the highest priority, so that's where He began. His next move was to divide the light from the darkness. The spiritual world is no different. First, Jesus becomes the Light of our life. Then He leads us out of darkness.

Then Jesus spoke to them again, saying, "I am the light of the world. He who follows Me shall not walk in darkness, but have the light of life" – John 8:12.

When I think of spiritual light, I first think of Jesus. He is the Creator of physical light, and He personifies spiritual light. Then I think of light existing within the realms of truth—of revelation, understanding, and wisdom. These living elements are found in the Spirit of the Lord, and they fill our lives with brilliant clarity. Such remarkable gifts, all wrapped up in Jesus, come to us from the Father of lights.

Every good gift and every perfect gift is from above, and comes down from the Father of lights, with whom there is no variation or shadow of turning – James 1:17.

At our invitation, the Light of God invades us and puts His stamp of salvation on our spirit—actually uniting with it. This can never be undone. Any time thereafter, when we partake of the Light, more darkness has to flee from our souls. Nourished by the Light, we grow and bloom and beautify our world.

As evangelists, preachers, teachers, prophets, intercessors, and more (every spiritual warrior), we have the heart of God, so we echo His words, *"Let there be light!"* We send it forth into murky hearts, dismal homes, oppressive relationships, evil environments, and to every place of darkness we encounter.

Because Christians are "one with the Lord" (1 Corinthians 6:17), we too are the light of the world (Matthew 5:14-15). Today, our individual flames are uniting. Choreographed by the Lord, they form a raging fire that is spreading throughout the Earth. Every day, more darkness is exposed. Truth is illumined and magnified. Enlightened choices are being made. And as always, we give God the glory.

Dear Lord, we love Your beautiful, holy Light. Please expose and remove every lingering shadow that is hiding in our souls. Please bless our families and friends with an increase of Your brilliant truth. Give us all a "spirit of wisdom and revelation" concerning You (Ephesians 1:17).

_____

_____

_____

_____

_____

_____

_____

_____

_____

_____

_____

_____

_____

Moving Closer

March 26, 2006

Christians move closer to the fullness of God with every time of testing. As long as we're obedient, we continually step to higher plateaus. Each new level is an excellent place to be—unless we stay there too long.

We cannot rush the refinement that is vital to our destiny, but neither should we master a small domain and plan to stay there forever. God wants us always moving closer to Him.

Mercy and grace will turn up the heat in our comfortable situation. Soon we'll be sweating and feeling faint—looking for ways to get relief. If you're like me, you may look to the left or step to the right, being full of bright ideas. But the temperature just keeps rising.

Now we've reached a critical point. Relief is actually near, and it will come in one of two ways. We can pridefully choose to stay where we are, seeking relief through familiar sources and using our own careful reasoning. The Refining Fire will back away, and His heat will slowly subside. *We must beware of making this choice.*

For My people have committed two evils: They have forsaken Me, the fountain of living waters, and hewn themselves cisterns— broken cisterns that can hold no water - Jeremiah 2:13.

The wise choice is to humbly bow before Jesus. We'll find sweet relief in His presence, where the clean scent of His love will soon revive us. Increased clarity will fortify our resolve, and newfound truth will enlarge our hope. When we open our eyes and look around, we'll discover that we've been moved again to higher ground.

Whom have I in heaven but You? And there is none upon earth that I desire besides You. My flesh and my heart fail; but God is the strength of my heart and my portion forever. For indeed, those who are far from You shall perish; You have destroyed all those who desert You for harlotry. But it is good for me to draw near to God; I have put my trust in the Lord God, that I may declare all Your works – Psalm 73:25-28.

110

Keep us near, Lord, and keep us always stepping higher. We find light and love and joy in Your presence. We move from glory to glory as we abide in You.

_____

_____

_____

_____

_____

_____

_____

_____

_____

_____

_____

_____

_____

_____

_____

_____

_____

_____

_____

Be Enriched

April 7, 2006

Some of us use blocking devices on our computers to deflect and minimize internet intrusions. We don't want to be swamped by a flood of unwelcome information. For similar reasons, we often block out spiritual information if it doesn't come from our personally approved sources. After all, we can only read so much, so shouldn't it be something we agree with? Well, not necessarily. This attitude of exclusion can be dangerous. The Holy Spirit urges us to seek *all* the wisdom He offers. He wants to reveal *every* truth that we need for victorious living (John 16:13).

Has your Christian environment become strict and narrow? Let me challenge you to branch out—always using the Word as a plumb line. Take a look at some things you've previously held at a distance.

Explore the value and purpose of today's prophetic movement. Dare to believe that God speaks through your dreams and that you can learn to interpret them. Read about the gift of healing and how it is active in the body of Christ today. Select one of the excellent books written about prayer, by those who effectively intercede. Carefully use the internet to discover some new and anointed Christian ministries.

> **And of His fullness we have all received, and grace for grace – John 1:16.**

Dare to embrace the "full gospel." Don't discard a particular truth because of family tradition or denominational taboos. The grace of God is rich and good. We need to drink every drop.

Having then gifts differing according to the grace that is given to us, let us use them: if prophecy, let us prophesy in proportion to our faith; or ministry, let us use it in our ministering; he who teaches, in teaching; he who exhorts, in exhortation; he who gives, with liberality; he who leads, with diligence; he who shows mercy, with cheerfulness. Let love be without hypocrisy. Abhor what is evil. Cling to what is good - Romans 12:6-9.

Thank You, Lord, for fullness of Your truth, for the rich depth of Your grace, and the sweetness of Your never-ending love. Help us to partake daily from the banquet You set before us.

_____

_____

_____

_____

_____

_____

_____

_____

_____

_____

_____

_____

_____

_____

_____

_____

_____

_____

With All Your Heart

October 22, 2006

Is there distance between you and God? And if so, does it seem okay? If both of your answers are "yes," then you have cause for concern. God wants Christians to love Him completely, and a casual acquaintance will not accomplish this. Extravagant love comes only through intimacy.

When you're in need of help or comfort, beware of choosing the charms of this world instead of the Lord. Please don't turn your back on the One who is Love Incarnate. Rise up and run after God! Seek Him with all your heart! He is the Special Prize to be won.

"And you shall love the Lord your God with all your heart, with all your soul, with all your mind, and with all your strength." This is the first commandment - Mark 12:30.

Your relationship with God may already be warm and cozy, but if He wants you even closer, you'll be wise to not resist. The Lord will go to great lengths to have His way within your heart.

Most of us stay too distant from You, dear Lord. Before another day goes by, reveal to us our desperate need for all that You are and all that You have for each of us. Please show us personal, practical ways to draw near.

No Longer a Servant

May 17, 2008

No longer do I call you servants, for a servant does not know what his master is doing; but I have called you friends, for all things that I heard from My Father I have made known to you - John 15:15.

You know you're a friend of God when He begins sharing His plans with you. The Holy Spirit told me an amazing secret a few weeks ago—on 4/5/08, to be exact. At first I felt a bit of pride, but only for a moment. Having a special secret between me and God that no other human knows is really the coolest thing. It's been a bonding experience at a whole new level. Because this secret will grow into a life-long venture, we have plenty of talking to do. *Oh my goodness!* The Lord and I have a big project together! I really am excited!

The secret has created a need to know much more. I've been shown the framework of something big, but I don't yet know the details. I'm certain the Lord will fill me in as we spend more time together. He has ideas, and I do too, so there will be much discussion. Yes, we'll talk together as cherished friends. Of course I don't consider my friendship with God to be one of equals. We're more like a Lion and a child. Nevertheless, we'll plot and plan (with roars and giggles), enjoying each other's company.

I've always felt good about God loving me, but being His friend is amazing.

My dearest friend, Jesus: Thank You for sharing Your plans with me— and for letting me play a major role in the drama that will unfold. You have added some jaw-dropping excitement to my otherwise ordinary life. I laugh when I think of our secret, and I smile when I think of You.

_____

_____

_____

_____

His Mercy Endures Forever

June 12, 2007

How many times have you remembered an episode of foolishness from your past, only to be overcome with gratitude for the Father's mercy? These unpleasant memories are stirred up by the enemy, but they serve to remind us of God's love and protection. His great compassion surrounded us in the past and even touched us before we were born. It is with us this very day. According to His word, God's mercy is with us forever.

Praise the Lord! Oh, give thanks to the Lord, for He is good! For His mercy endures forever - Psalm 106:1.

When my battle with sin isn't going too well, then I find myself saying, *"Please don't give up on me, Lord."* This plea is always sincere, so I know I'll receive the mercy I need.

God's enduring mercy is a large part of our Christian foundation. It certainly filled the Father's heart when He sent Jesus to the cross. So on those days when we imagine we've used up every bit of God's patience, then it's good to call for His never-ending mercies.

Through the Lord's mercies we are not consumed because His compassions fail not. They are new every morning; great is Your faithfulness - Lamentations 3:22-23.

Dearest merciful God, we are utterly dependent on Your compassion. When nobody else understands or cares, You stand before us with outstretched arms, calling us close, and giving us another chance. We thank You from the depths of our being! We will praise You through eternity.

God Can

October 31, 2008

God has no expectations of our human nature. He knows it will always fail when the pressure is on, and our buttons are pushed. This flesh will never get any better.

The only way to consistently act in a Godly manner is to abide in Christ and be filled each day with His Spirit. Then, whenever we're given a clear command, we'll also have the power to accomplish it. Whether it be to move a mountain or simply to speak of something God has done, the Lord is always available to work through us.

We can't mend relationships that have come undone—but God can. We can't protect our families and country from every single enemy—but God can. We can't heal the sick or raise the dead or save a soul from hell—but God can. All of this and more, God wants to do through us.

But you shall receive power when the Holy Spirit has come upon you; and you shall be witnesses to Me in Jerusalem, and in all Judea and Samaria, and to the end of the earth - Acts 1:8.

We want to be bright and shining ambassadors of Your power, dear Lord. The world is full of opportunity for Your strength to be displayed. Just point us in the right direction. Show us which need is ours to focus on today. Then let the fire of Your presence be released through our hands. Let Your love and grace flow from our lips. Let the needs of today be completely met.

_____

_____

_____

_____

_____

_____

_____

Disciples of the Lord

January 14, 2007

By definition, disciples are being *disciplined*. Christian disciples are taken through levels of training that others would never submit to. Committed to our leader, the Lord Jesus Christ, we are "soldiers of the cross"—always marching to the clear cadence of victory.

A disciple is not above his teacher, but everyone who is perfectly trained will be like his teacher - Luke 6:40.

Jesus faced adversity, and so must we. Hardship is a refining tool in the hand of God. A life of ease will never produce His desired results. When things get rough, we're taught to respond with power and love and a sound mind (2 Timothy 1:7). We learn to pray for those who mistreat us (Matthew 5:44) and count it all joy when we fall into various trials (James 1:2). We're commanded to be strong and courageous (Joshua 1:9), never reacting with fear because no weapon formed against us will prosper (Isaiah 54:17). Truly, these mature responses can only be learned through recurrent times of difficulty.

We are works in progress who sometimes stumble and fall—and too often we complain. But if we cooperate with our Leader and yield to His supremacy, then one day soon we'll be valiant forces who storm the gates of hell!

Know then in your heart that as a man disciplines his son, so the Lord your God disciplines you. Observe the commands of the Lord your God, walking in his ways and revering him – Deuteronomy 8:5-6.

El Gibbor, our Mighty God, please open our eyes. Let us see Your loving hand of discipline as it frames our circumstances. Help us submit to Your training. Be strong in us to carry out Your commands. Let love compel us in every battle as it compelled You on the cross.

The River of Life

September 27, 2009

There is a river whose streams shall make glad the city of God, the holy place of the tabernacle of the Most High - Psalm 46:4.

The river of God brings life to all who drink from it. In Ezekiel 47:9, we read that *"...everything will live wherever the river goes."* Now how does this apply to us? I believe it means that everything touched by God will be filled with *life!* If something has died, then the water of God will make it *alive!* It means that in God's presence is found the powerful, beautiful life that Jesus bought for us on the cross.

Amazingly, we don't have to look very far to find this river. It freely flows from the presence of God within us. Yes, friends, we are vessels of power and LIFE!

Maybe you're not well-acquainted with the Treasure you carry around each day. Maybe you've been distracted by the world and deceived by Satan's lies. But this can be easily changed by spending time each day in the Word, in worship and in prayer. Before long, you'll be ready to leave the shallows. Soon you'll be diving into the depths of God, bringing His life to those who wait so timidly on the shore.

Please, Lord, give us a strong thirst for Your living water. We thank You for this refreshing, supernatural gift and all it includes. Thank You for Your love, Your healing, and all of Your provision. Thank You for Your dynamic presence within us. We never want to be without You.

_____

_____

_____

_____

_____

_____

Comfort and Joy

March 9, 2007

All of us want to feel safe and comfortable. Depending on our personalities and backgrounds, we have unique needs, even in our options for personal solace. Some common "comforters" are food, television, shopping, talking to friends, and even work. This short list has only scratched the surface because we are quite creative when it comes to pacifying ourselves.

The problem with our self-comforting is that overindulgence has negative side-effects and repercussions. Even so, we may continue to indulge because of our genuine need for relief from the pressures of this world. So what's the solution? Undeniably, God Himself is the Answer.

**You will show me the path of life; in Your presence is fullness of joy; at Your right hand are pleasures forevermore –
Psalm 16:11.**

"Fullness of joy" and "pleasures forevermore" sound wonderful. So, why do we choose chocolate bars or new gadgets when we can indulge in the pleasures of God?

The Lord has proven Himself to be faithful, time and time again, so why don't we give Him a chance to lift us up and away from our destructive habits? The next time we're tempted by the media, the phone, or an unhealthy snack, let's instead retreat to a quiet place and trust that God is right there with us. We can praise Him and thank Him, then quietly wait for His enriching, satisfying presence.

But the water that I shall give him will become in him a fountain of water springing up into everlasting life" – John 4:13-14.

Please comfort us with Your truth, dear Lord, and revive us with Your love. You have created us with an inner void that can only be filled by You. Help us to keep the "lesser things" of this world in their proper place.

120

The One Who Collects My Tears

December 13, 2006

One of my favorite things about God is His patience with my human frailty. He doesn't belittle me for being weak. With genuine love, God never tires of hearing about my struggles and emotions. If I tell Him about someone's unkindness to me, He doesn't interrupt to say, *"That happened to me one time. Let me tell you about it."* Instead, He listens to my story with loving attention and concern.

You keep track of all my sorrows. You have collected all my tears in your bottle. You have recorded each one in your book - Psalm 56:8 NLT.

How can I help but praise Him—this wonderful One who collects my tears in a bottle?

I never feel ignored by God or insignificant to Him. In fact, I know that He's delighted with me. It doesn't bother Him the slightest bit that I'm "only a woman" or that according to worldly measures I have little influence or money. God is the One who enjoys my company, even though others may consider me irrelevant and of little consequence. He's the One who declares my value when society says I haven't achieved enough.

The Lord is my strength and my shield; my heart trusts in him, and I am helped. My heart leaps for joy and I will give thanks to him in song - Psalm 28:7 NIV.

We love You, Lord, because You loved us first. You loved us enough to die on the cross and pay for our sins! One day we will comprehend the fullness of Your love. But until then, we thank You for listening to our stories, saving our tears, and intervening whenever we ask—in the most amazing ways. You are absolutely awesome!

Gateways

October 14, 2009

When we go through personal trials, the Word comes alive with new revelation that fits our situation. The love and power and deliverance of God take on new significance. The bigger the tribulation, the greater is God's Word to meet it. Trials are uncomfortable and often frightening, but they are always gateways leading deeper into God. Because of this, we can embrace our difficulties and *rejoice* in them (1 Peter 1:6).

You are my hiding place; You shall preserve me from trouble; You shall surround me with songs of deliverance - Psalm 32:7.

Being "surrounded" by God is the perfect place to be. A trial can't be too much to bear with the arms of the Lord wrapped tightly around us. With His whispers of love, how can we not be courageous? With His kisses of truth, how can we not be bold?

...let all those rejoice who put their trust in You; let them ever shout for joy, because You defend them; Let those also who love Your name be joyful in You. For You, O Lord, will bless the righteous; with favor You will surround him as with a shield - Psalm 5:11-12.

Dear sweet Lord, we thank You for making gateways into Your heart. Please give us courage to pass through these trials that lead to You.

_____

_____

_____

_____

_____

_____

_____

Resting in God

May 28, 2007

Learning to rest in the care of our loving God sounds like an easy task. But this can be hard for Christians to attain if we've ever had confidence in our own abilities. We don't intentionally elevate ourselves to a position of not needing God, but the enemy will trick us into doing just that. We're given one "good idea" after another, and we quickly get to work, using our natural talents.

Meanwhile, God is working to show us our genuine need for Him, no matter how long it takes. Those talents that helped us in the past may now begin to fail us. People we considered to be friends may start to back away. Everything we trusted in before we met the Lord will now be exposed as unreliable. At this point, we're wary of any "good ideas," and we're ready for God to be in charge. At least we *think* we're ready.

To successfully rest in the Lord and receive His help, we must first get to know Him. It took time to conquer the habit of trusting in ourselves, and now it will take even more time to arrive at trusting God completely. But we need not worry. Our Lord has a way of putting us in settings that make us wonder what we can expect from Him—and then He gladly shows us.

A relationship grows one step at a time. Our trust in God's love and His care for us increases every time we're tested. Each victory is celebrated with joy, and then we move on to another faith-building trial. Day by day, year after year, we fall more in love with our faithful God and His superior ways. Over time, because we love Him and trust Him, we can easily rest in Him.

I have set the Lord always before me; because He is at my right hand I shall not be moved. Therefore my heart is glad, and my glory rejoices; my flesh also will rest in hope - Psalm 16:8-9.

Don't let us fall short, dear Lord, of finding perfect rest in You. Let us see clearly Your desire to promote us and to pour Your glory upon us. Thank You for the intricate, customized paths that You've prepared for every beloved child—paths that reveal the wonders of You.

123

How Sweet Is the Joy

March 22, 2010

Oh, how sweet is the joy that comes from feeling God's love—from knowing He's pleased with our progress—from receiving personal words of direction! I'm feeling this joy today because God has greatly encouraged me.

I will instruct you and teach you in the way you should go; I will guide you with My eye – Psalm 32:8.

My encouragement came during a time of prayer. I asked the Lord a specific question which He didn't answer. But He quickly addressed the root of the matter which was a lot more important. The answer came as a mental image of an hour glass. Along with the image came a clear understanding of what it meant. God was telling me that what He had promised two years ago will come in His sovereign timing. He hasn't changed His mind.

I began pondering the contrast between this time of joy and some recent times of mild depression. Obviously, joy comes for Christians when we're feeling loved and accepted by the Lord. Depression can come from the illusion that He has withdrawn His love. The enemy subtly tricks us into believing we're a disappointment to God. Because these are not clear, concise thoughts, the associated feelings can linger for weeks before we question their source.

The truth is, God *always* loves us. He is extremely patient and never gives up. He's promised to finish what He has begun (Philippians 1:6).

God wants us feeling good about being His. He desires that we're always filled with His joy and His strength (Nehemiah 8:10). If we fall into a slump of negativity, our friendship with God holds the cure. Spending time in the Word is actually spending time with the Lord, and believing the Word is believing in His character. Being delighted by both our time and our trust, God will draw increasingly near.

And so it happened just as the Scriptures say: "Abraham believed God, and God counted him as righteous because of his faith." He was even called the friend of God – James 2:23 NLT.

Dear Lord, we count Your friendship as precious indeed. The way You relate to us is a model for us to follow with others. As always, You raise the bar high, and then You call us upward. We will follow You forever on the lofty path You've prepared.

_____

_____

_____

_____

_____

_____

_____

_____

_____

_____

_____

_____

_____

_____

_____

_____

_____

What a Friend I Have in Jesus

April 1, 2009

I love that Jesus is my best friend. Human friends will sometimes disappoint because, after all, they're human. But Jesus is always faithfully by my side, and He's absolutely perfect. He's proven His love for me over and over again—first at the cross, then every day thereafter.

Jesus cares how I feel. When I'm upset about something, the Lord doesn't fuss at me for being emotional. Instead, He reminds me of the truth I need to hear, beginning with "I love you." He also likes to share in my happiness.

Jesus wants the very best for me. He teaches and encourages—always guiding me toward His purest blessings and highest purpose.

Jesus loves the ones I love. When I pray for the special people in my life, I am assured that Jesus loves them more than I do, and He will do "whatever it takes" to bring them into His Kingdom. *Oh, how good You are, dear Lord!*

Jesus is fun. The more I get to know Him, the more delighted I am with Jesus' personality. He has a great sense of humor, and I find myself laughing out loud at His jokes—the kind that are shared by friends. He also surprises me with meaningful "little things."

Jesus is awe-inspiring. All matters of life and love are wrapped in His arms. It's great to have such an awesome, powerful friend to hang out with—one who always lifts me higher.

Your steadfast love, O Lord, extends to the heavens, your faithfulness to the clouds – Psalm 36:5 ESV.

Dear Lord Jesus, You are the Friend that none of us deserve but each of us need. You are beyond our wildest dreams. Thank You for all You are and everything You do. We look forward to eternity.

_____

_____

When We're Thirsty

July 10, 2006

I witnessed a delightful backyard scene today. My lawn sprinkler was set to oscillate between a crabapple tree and a newly planted shrub. From a kitchen window, I noticed some cardinals perched in the small, water-soaked tree. Thinking they would soon fly away to avoid the oncoming spray, I laughed out loud when I realized they were actually waiting to get wet! They seemed to enjoy being washed as they happily drank from the leaves. When the shower reversed and moved to the hawthorn bush, some of the birds flew there to be sprinkled again right away.

It's important to know that under a tree in my front yard sit three perfectly good birdbaths that are always filled with water. Apparently, cardinals prefer the sprinkled drops that flow cool and fresh, straight from the well.

Just as the backyard birds position themselves to drink the purest water, so should we strive to be refreshed by the Living Water of God. We must fly to where we know He is. And if we see Him move, then we should quickly follow.

...As the deer pants for the water brooks, so pants my soul for You, O God. My soul thirsts for God, for the living God – Psalm 42:1-2.

Thank You, Lord, for speaking so vividly through Your creation. We thank You for being our Living Water. Please submerge us daily in Your wondrous, cooling depths. Refresh us with Your love.

_____

_____

_____

_____

_____

_____

When the Time Is Right

April 22, 2006

Are you oppressed? Poor? Discouraged? Are you dissatisfied with your life and yearning to realize the dreams that God has placed in your heart? Well, it's time to look up! The Lord truly does have a plan for your future.

The minute that you submit to God's hand on your life, He begins preparing you to walk at much higher levels. You become a high-priority "work in progress," with extensive transformation taking place. Please don't be alarmed or dejected when God's methods become rigorous.

Surprisingly, experience with oppression is quite valuable. Dealing with tyrants and bullies will fine-tune your skills in spiritual warfare and draw you deeper into the Word—into the heart of God. Certain truths are only understood by the "poor in circumstance." The presence of God is most often found by those who know they need Him. The "fellowship of Jesus' suffering" will almost always precede His resurrection power (Philippians 3:10).

Lowly conditions are tools in the hand of God. Each discomfort has a divine purpose, and the distress is only intended for a season of growth. Our Lord of grace and mercy desires for us to be Christ-like more than He desires for us to be comfortable. As we relinquish our sinful ways and submit to His methods of refinement, God will move mountains on our behalf.

"For the oppression of the poor, for the sighing of the needy, now I will arise," says the Lord; "I will set him in the safety for which he yearns" - Psalm 12:5.

Yes, yes, yes! God wants to bless us in many ways, but only when the time is right. He doesn't want the gifts to distract us from knowing Him, and there may be other weighty considerations that we're unaware of. We need to patiently trust in His wisdom.

Let's never forget that Jesus came to set us completely free from bondage, including all types of poverty (Isaiah 61:1). He came to bless us so we can bless others. Very soon, on a special day of destiny, God's glory will fall upon us and shine brightly through us for all the world to see (Isaiah 60:1-3).

Dear Lord, we thank You for transforming us. Please help us to see how we are blessed by You this very day. Don't let us despise the small beginnings (Zechariah 4:10). Help us to patiently wait for the larger blessings to come. Let us always be aware of Your loving hand upon us.

_____

_____

_____

_____

_____

_____

_____

_____

_____

_____

_____

_____

_____

_____

_____

_____

_____

_____

_____

Totally Dependent

August 23, 2015

Who is this coming up from the wilderness, leaning upon her beloved? – Song of Solomon 8:5.

Many Christians today are "coming up from the wilderness." As we lean on our beloved Jesus, we find ourselves in love with Him, in awe of Him, and totally dependent on Him. We walk hopefully and expectantly into the future, hand in hand with our glorious Lord. Upon our frail human shoulders rests a garment of many colors, woven with luminous thread that was spun from truth gleaned in the desert. The strands of truth form a beautiful tapestry of promise that we know will be fulfilled—a mantle of purpose that God has lovingly prepared.

Blessed is the man whose strength is in You, whose heart is set on pilgrimage. As they pass through the valley of Baca, they make it a spring; the rain also covers it with pools. They go from strength to strength; each one appears before God in Zion – Psalm 84:5-7.

A vibrant, emerging sector of Christianity is composed of those who have met with God in the wastelands and the valleys—whose hearts were carefully transformed in the dry and rocky places—who made a spring in their desert because of His love.

Are you one of these radiant believers? Have you walked through painful, desolate, difficult years, and in them formed an intimate, unbreakable bond with the Light of Life—a bond that has value far beyond calculation? I have some friends who have made this wilderness journey, as well as myself, so I know that each trip is different. There is no map. There are no shortcuts. But the Word is always near, shining ever so brightly on the unique route that God prepares—the road that leads us into the depths of Himself.

How sweet are Your words to my taste, sweeter than honey to my mouth!... Thy word is a lamp unto my feet, and a light unto my path – Psalm 119:103, 105 KJV.

Today, as I lean on my Beloved, I still see rocks to avoid and protruding limbs to dodge. Enemies continue to hide in the bushes. But at this point in my journey with the Lord, I lean hard enough for full support. Foes may startle me, but Jesus quickly deflects all fiery darts of fear. He squeezes my hand and points to the horizon, saying, "Look! The promise is almost here."

The eternal God is your refuge...underneath are the everlasting arms; He will thrust out the enemy from before you, and will say, 'Destroy!' – Deuteronomy 33:27.

If your time in the wilderness is just beginning, the best thing to do—the only wise option—is to take the hand of God and never let go. The next thing to do is toss your heavy burden of pride into the evening campfire, and let it be consumed. (Pride will only cause trouble, for you and others.) Share your ideas with the Lord, but always submit to His direction. Talk to Him about your problems, and listen carefully to His response. Keep holding tightly to Jesus' hand so diversions and "shortcuts" won't seduce you. Remember, there is a purpose for this journey that will stretch into eternity.

Oh, taste and see that the Lord is good; blessed is the man who trusts in Him! Oh, fear the Lord, you His saints! There is no want to those who fear Him. The young lions lack and suffer hunger; but those who seek the Lord shall not lack any good thing – Psalm 34:8-10.

Thank You, Lord, for seasons in the wilderness that draw us deeper into Your beautiful heart. Within the barren wastelands, all pretense is dropped and exchanged for fellowship with You. In the wilderness, our world is shaken and torn, but You stay with us in our trouble, holding us close and secure.

_____

_____

Surrounded

April 12, 2006

Three of my favorite things are springtime, rain, and Saturday mornings. I remember a special time of being blessed by having these three events coincide. Rain fell and thunder rumbled from early morning through mid-afternoon. During a break in the weather, I photographed stormy skies above the wooded horizon. Sparkling drops of water, clinging to petals and leaves, are now preserved in digital files.

Rain brings a welcome respite from the ordinary. Gently softening the world around us, it cleans and renews all that it touches. This mild spring storm brought awakening to the land and peace to my spirit.

Because rain is all encompassing, it makes me aware of the same attribute of God. I see Him in the darkened clouds, and I watch as He ruffles the trees. I breath in His stormy fragrance and marvel as He exhales water across my lawn. I smile when Adonai gently rattles the vent on my roof. I love being captured by His presence—completely surrounded and thoroughly safe.

In the matters of life, God always hovers over me and often hems me in. He arranges my days, so I can't escape the growth He has planned for me. Though I'm frightened at times by being constrained, I remember that He is the same wonderful God who inhabits the wind and the rain. Enclosed in His purpose, safe in His arms, I find peace in His mighty, masterful ways.

As the mountains surround Jerusalem, so the Lord surrounds His people from this time forth and forever - Psalm 125:2.

Dear Lord, we thank You for surrounding us. Our captivity is sweet because You are the good and holy Captor. With only our best in mind, You enclose us in Your love.

Lord, You Are My Life!

September 17, 2016

I said to the Lord, *"You are my Life."*

And the Lord replied, *"Yes, I AM!"*

I said to the Lord,

> *"You are the wise and wonderful Voice I hear.*
> *You are the Light on every rocky path.*
> *You are the Truth, always standing steadfast.*
> *You are the faithful Rock I lean on.*
> *You are my Shelter in every storm.*
> *You are the Holy One who lifts me high.*
> *You are the Goodness and Kindness I crave.*
> *You are the Friend who helps me walk on water.*
> *You are the Favor, always surrounding me.*
> *You are my wealthy Kinsman Redeemer.*
> *You are the Answer to everything I will ever need.*
> *You are the Grace and Love I cannot live without."*

And the Lord replied, *"Yes, I AM! Always and forever!"*

_____

_____

_____

_____

_____

_____

_____

_____

DESTINY

We Can All Be Heroes

April 1, 2006

Have you imagined being a hero like David—killing the local giants? Or being installed as "God's person in high places," just like Joseph was? Do you envision traveling the land like Paul, shining a light wherever you go?

These men were just as human as you and I, but each was ordained for a special purpose. Each had a role to play in God's unfolding plan. The Bible clearly portrays their weaknesses, and in spite of these, they rose to prominent positions in history. It was not human strength but the power and grace of God that carried them over obstacles and all the way to victory.

I'm certain that all the leading roles have not been taken. God has glorious plans for every single one of us. Whether high profile or quietly covert, our assignments have huge potential—we're each intended for greatness. Yes, God is calling us all to be "heroes of the faith." With Christ in us, our destinies are significant.

Both riches and honor come from you, and you rule over all. In your hand are power and might, and in your hand it is to make great and to give strength to all. And now we thank you, our God, and praise your glorious name – 1 Chronicles 29:12-13 ESV.

You, dear Lord, have created us for roles that are substantial. You've placed in our hearts a desire to arise from mediocrity and to do great things in Your kingdom. Thank You for living within us to carry out the amazing feats that lie ahead.

_____

_____

_____

_____

_____

The Dreams of God

September 22, 2015

"In the beginning," God had a very big dream. *Then He spoke it into existence!* Because God is a dreamer, then so are His people. Our enduring, long-term dreams most often begin in the heart of God, then He plants the seed of His holy desire into our thoughts. From there they grow and expand, taking root throughout our being.

Several years ago, the Lord planted a very large dream in my heart. I know that one day soon I'll be shouting about its tangible reality. But until then, my testimony is a quiet one of walking with God on a well-lit path of faith, hope, and truth.

I wait for the LORD, my soul waits, and in His word I do hope. My soul waits for the Lord more than those who watch for the morning—Yes, more than those who watch for the morning – Psalm 130:5-6.

The Holy Spirit does not abide in us to be unobtrusive and silent. He shares His vision with a determined voice of passion. The seed of God's dreams planted deep within us brings growth and transformation. We're destined to be the "good soil" that is required for dreams to materialize. Once a dream becomes as real and dear to us as it is to God, then even our doubts will push us to the throne of grace where we find confirmation and assurance, as often as we ask. This is especially true with dreams that are substantial and far-reaching. Our Father is eager to help us believe for the impossible.

I want to stress that we must *choose* to believe—sometimes on a daily or hourly basis. Believing is imperative, but it's also impossible apart from being immersed in the word of God. The Word will water our faith and keep our dream alive.

The LORD will guide you continually, and satisfy your soul in drought, and strengthen your bones; you shall be like a watered garden, and like a spring of water, whose waters do not fail – Isaiah 58:11.

Before God's will can be done on Earth, His word must be embraced and proclaimed by us. As we are inspired by the Spirit, we must declare relevant truth over our assigned domains and over our dreams. These words can be scripture, or they can be the personal words of promise that God has carefully made known to us. Both are the mighty sword of the Spirit (Ephesians 6:17).

God loves to be reminded of His word. He loves to hear it echo powerfully through the chambers of His creation, making the powers of darkness bow to its authority.

I'm convinced that God dreams of the days when He will elevate each of us—of specific times when He will joyfully crown us with promotion or open a door of miraculous blessing. I believe He dreams of the look in our eyes when the promise finally appears.

The dreams we share with You, dear Lord, will soon be seen upon the Earth. We rest in You, knowing that Your timing is flawless, and Your faithfulness is beyond reproach.

_____

_____

_____

_____

_____

_____

_____

_____

_____

Painters of Destiny

February 12, 2014

God keeps teaching me about prayer because He has blessings and changes ahead for my life that are not optional—neither in His estimation or in mine. *These things simply have to be.* Therefore, I'm learning to fight for what is mine, and I'm teaching others to do the same.

Spiritual warfare always revolves around God's word, but how we view ourselves as warriors has many variables. During a recent time of prayer, the Lord showed me a steep mountain. Near the tip of the rocky peak was a natural basin filled with water that was transparent but also dark. I was reminded of the water that artists use to clean the paint from their brushes. If enough colors are used, this water becomes gray or brown. God's message for me in this vision was that "He and I together are painters of destiny." His Living Word, administered by me in prayer, will create some bright and beautiful futures.

This message applies to anyone who has a need or sees a need. We can all use God's word as a palette of life-giving color to paint His will into being. As you read the following familiar verse about God's plans, please hear the passion in His voice. He wants us to *believe* so we will pray.

"For I know the plans that I have for you," declares the Lord, "plans for welfare and not for calamity, to give you a future and a hope" – Jeremiah 29:11 NASB.

The word of God holds tremendous power, but it is only released when we pick up this "paint" and apply it with our brush of faith. The Holy Spirit selects the perfect hues by reminding us of relevant scripture or whispering personal words. *Seriously.* When God picks the color, we know it's going to be right. A life is going to change.

If you abide in Me, and My words abide in you, ask whatever you wish, and it will be done for you – John 15:7 ESV.

Storing up God's word in our hearts is like stocking the shelves of an artist's studio with the most expensive, highest quality paints that exist.

Rare and surprising color can flow from consecrated tubes and jars, and then be applied to the canvas of someone's destiny—*if* we embrace the assignment.

Dear Lord God, we thank You for Your beautiful Word—for the artistry held within it. Thank You for the loving plans You have for all of us. We're humble apprentices in Your grand studio of prayer, and we truly want to learn. Please help us to hear Your voice when You tell us which colors of paint are needed and which brushes we should use. We want to do our part in bringing Your will to Earth. We want the destiny of Your people to unfold in radiant, living color.

_____

_____

_____

_____

_____

_____

_____

_____

_____

_____

_____

_____

_____

_____

Destiny Has a Voice

April 21, 2013

Destiny pulls on us from the future, pushes us from the past and hems us in on the left and the right. Destiny has a voice: "I am the will of God. I am found in the heart of God. Pursue Me every day."

...I press on, that I may lay hold of that for which Christ Jesus has also laid hold of me – Philippians 3:12.

From the future, Destiny* beckons, "Please come to Me. I have an excellent plan for your life. I have holy purpose that calls for your participation."

From our past, Destiny urges, "You go on ahead. Don't look back at your mistakes. Keep moving forward into the many good works that I've prepared for you."

From the left, Destiny warns, "I know it looks like fun over here, but it's only an illusion that leads to sorrow. Just keep moving forward on My straight and narrow path where you'll find peace, joy and all types of prosperity."

From the right, Destiny cautions, "Yes, there is plenty of 'good' to do over here, but it's 'works of the flesh' and not what I have planned for you. Turning this way will waste your precious time."

Destiny calls to us loudly from the Word—inspiring, directing and transforming every Christian. Destiny woos and captures us, but never violates our free will:

For I am confident of this very thing, that He who began a good work in you will perfect it until the day of Christ Jesus – Philippians 1:6.

Destiny requires that we have confidence in the Word—to use it as a mighty sword against every enemy we encounter, and to shape the future with bold decrees when the Spirit inspires. Destiny is pleased when God's voice becomes our voice, proving that our hearts are in agreement:

And take.....the sword of the Spirit, which is the word of God; praying always with all prayer and supplication in the Spirit... - Ephesians 6:17-18.

Destiny appeals to our hearts and minds through vision. Nighttime dreams, waking visions, inspired ideas and other types of enlightenment come by the Spirit of God. This revelation brings the focus we need while traveling rocky roads ahead:

For the vision is yet for the appointed time; it hastens toward the goal and it will not fail. Though it tarries, wait for it; for it will certainly come, it will not delay – Habakkuk 2:3 NASB.

Destiny insists that we're born again and abiding in Christ:

I am the vine, you are the branches. He who abides in Me, and I in him, bears much fruit; for without Me you can do nothing – John 15:5.

Dear Lord God, thank You for being our Destiny. No person, place or thing can measure up to the wonders of who You are. Nothing even comes close. Thank You for the purpose we find when abiding in You. Your voice imparts strategy, hope and power. You adorn us with relevance and significance. Our future is rich and bright because You are rich and bright.

* Our destiny is in God, so I take artistic license and treat the word as a proper name.

_____

_____

_____

_____

_____

I Will Do a New Thing

October 17, 2015

The normal Christian life is not without challenges. Most of us have lived through truly difficult times. Today, our circumstances might be improved, but the past can still cause trouble, without us even being aware. Negative words from bygone years may cast a large shadow on our lives:

> *Just accept the way things are. People rarely change.*
>
> *Don't expect too much. This is how it will always be.*
>
> *You had your chance, and you blew it. It's too late now.*
>
> *You did a terrible thing, and you should be ashamed.*
>
> *You're not special enough to do anything significant.*

These messages don't arrive as clearly spoken words. If they did, we would probably reject them right away because they conflict with scripture. Instead, they come from a dark file in our storehouse of memories—the ones that have lingered and evolved within us, becoming destructive attitudes and misguided emotions. Without our conscious permission, these sentiments undermine our faith in God and His word. We may believe what the Spirit and the Word tell us, but it's often a struggle to do so. We know that God is faithful and good, but way down deep, we don't expect miracles to come our way. The little stuff, maybe, but nothing big.

Again—these negative attitudes are not conscious choices. They are hidden mindsets that can permeate our present and spoil our future.

But God has good news for us! Today, all things are new! If we abide in Christ, the past has lost its power to control us in negative ways (2 Corinthians 5:17). God has removed our "ashes" and given us beauty in their place (Isaiah 61:3)! We can apply this powerful truth to every aspect of our lives—beginning with our thoughts.

Do not remember the former things, nor consider the things of old. Behold, I will do a new thing, now it shall spring forth; shall you not know it? I will even make a road in the wilderness and rivers in the desert. The beast of the field will honor Me, the jackals and the ostriches, because I give waters in the wilderness and rivers in the desert, to give drink to My people, My chosen. This people I have formed for Myself; they shall declare My praise – Isaiah 43:18-21.

Let's stop right now, and ask the Lord to expose any disparaging voices that are calling from previous years. If we hear them clearly, then we can reject them once and for all as lies.

Thank You, Lord, for Your powerful Presence within us. Please shine Your light in every place where deception may be hiding. We only want Your vibrant, life-changing truth.

_____

_____

_____

_____

_____

_____

_____

_____

_____

_____

Looking Ahead

December 27, 2010

Our walk with the Lord may be close and sweet, but all around us we see life being touched by sin. Destructive words are spoken, and selfish behavior gives off a stench that is difficult to ignore. These things used to upset me and take control of my thoughts, but now I rarely fret about the actions of other people. The Lord has even set me free from being overly concerned about my own behavior.

No matter who committed the sin, it is something to pray about and then forget about. We shouldn't keep looking back. We must not allow the problems of yesterday to have power over our minds and emotions today, allowing the sins of others to wound us repeatedly, or letting our own sin condemn us. Above all, we mustn't let our sinful past entice us to return. Looking back isn't the way of the Lord, so we must always resist this temptation.

Do you remember what happened to Lot's wife? After being warned by the rescuing angel to only look ahead, the foolish woman couldn't resist looking back. This event in Genesis is highly symbolic—a warning for us to heed.

But Lot's wife looked back as she was following behind him, and she turned into a pillar of salt – Genesis 19:26 NLT.

Whether they're logos words from the Bible or rhema words directly from the Spirit, God's promises are most certainly ahead of us and not behind.

A short time ago I was resisting an attack of repeated negative thoughts. They began the previous day when someone showed me disrespect. I had already forgiven the person, but the disruptive thoughts kept coming. I needed help, so I asked the Lord to advise me. He reminded me that whether the offense occurred five minutes ago or ten years ago, I must leave it behind me where it belongs. He told me that if Satan can keep my thoughts focused on an upsetting event of the past, then he'll effectively have me "stuck" in that place and time. (Lot's wife was stopped in her tracks; unable to take another step.) If I choose to remember offences from the past, then I am reliving these occasions, allowing them continued influence on me and others.

After reviewing the highly destructive effects of looking backward, the Lord enlightened me about the blessings of looking ahead—to Him and His holy purpose. Speaking into my thoughts, He revealed: *"Prophetic power resides even in your thinking, so the practice of looking ahead to Me and My word will stir up Your faith and thereby hasten the arrival of all that is good."*

May the LORD God of your fathers make you a thousand times more numerous than you are, and bless you as He has promised you! - Deuteronomy 1:11.

We have a choice: We can follow Satan's lead and dwell in the past, or we can keep our eyes on Jesus, the One who always calls us forward— onward and upward to the place in His plan where we belong.

Dear Lord, we thank You for putting our eyes in the front of our heads and not in the back. You don't dwell in the past, so neither should we. Please keep leading us forward with Your captivating presence. Lead us to places of enlargement. Lead us straight to where our destiny resides.

_____

_____

_____

_____

_____

_____

_____

While We Are Waiting

January 10, 2011

Joseph waited thirteen years to see the fulfillment of his God-given dreams. These were not easy years, by any stretch of the imagination. First, Joseph endured a crushing betrayal by his brothers. Then he coped with being a household slave and finally with imprisonment in a dungeon. Just when he saw some light at the end of this tunnel, Joseph was compelled to undergo two more years of confinement. All this happened while he was "waiting on the Lord."

Most Christians see the glory of God revealed when Pharaoh positioned Joseph as second-in-command over "all the land of Egypt" (Genesis 41:41). But we should also see the glory of God revealed through Joseph's attitude in the preceding thirteen years.

Joseph was given a preview of his destiny through two related dreams, but right away, the young man's faith was tested. One day he was freely roaming the plains as a youthful shepherd, and the next day he was a slave—all because of his brothers' jealousy. I'm certain that Joseph shed many tears. He surely poured out his heart to the Lord about the injustice done to him. Remember that Joseph was a man, just like us, with a heart of human flesh. And when he turned to the Lord for encouragement, he undoubtedly received it. Inside the prison, God sustained Joseph and gave him authority over many other men. He worked powerfully and thoroughly, preparing Joseph for the promotion that was ahead.

The years of Joseph's captivity resulted in a beautiful testimony. The glory of God rested upon this prisoner, causing him to excel at whatever task was before him—first in Potiphar's home, and then in the depths of a dungeon.

Blessed is the man whose strength is in You, whose heart is set on pilgrimage. As they pass through the Valley of Baca, they make it a spring; the rain also covers it with pools. They go from strength to strength; each one appears before God in Zion – Psalm 84:5-7.

Joseph lived in the "Valley of Baca" (the valley of weeping) for quite a while, and we see that his difficult years were not wasted. He could

148

easily have written a best-selling book about using the "lemons of life" to make sweet lemonade. Joseph's recipe might be something like this:

One very large lemon (a time of tribulation, overseen by God)
One quart water (from the life-giving river of God)
One cup sugar (the sweet and potent promise of a dream)

Joseph went from "strength to strength" as he walked with God in the valley, and so must we. Instead of complaining about our troubles, let's praise the Lord, then ask Him for encouraging words of purpose and direction.

While we are waiting on You, dear Lord, let everything we touch become a spring that others may drink from and be renewed. Let Your rain fill our valley with deep, clear pools. Let the light of Your glory rest upon us today.

_____

_____

_____

_____

_____

_____

_____

_____

_____

_____

_____

Will You Glorify the Lord?

March 8, 2010

What is the vision that guides you today? Are you fearfully watching the chaos and violence? Or do you focus with hope on the power and promise of God? If you find yourself afraid because of persistent "bad reports," then let this push you toward God's truth instead of pulling you into the demonic mire of despair.

God has not forsaken us. His Holy word still outranks the enemy's spiteful chatter. His benevolent plans still override every evil scheme. Immersing ourselves in scripture will increase our faith and discernment, but fear will push us into foolish error. The Word always brings revelation, while fear brings distortion and lies.

God has given us a choice. We can open our eyes to watch Him work. We can turn our ears to hear His voice. Or, we can join the masses who are deceived.

Will you glorify the Lord through faith, or will you discredit Him through fear?

Christians are destined to shine with the light of God's glory. The enemy knows this and is working overtime to tarnish our lamps and snuff out the fire within. In my personal experience, every time I take a significant step toward God, the forces of hell arrive to push me back. But the Spirit has taught me to expect these attacks and ward them off with faith. I know that you can do this too. The following precepts will help:

- Put on the whole armor of God (Ephesians 6:10-18).

- Remember all that God has promised, both in the Bible and in His personal words to you. Keep a detailed journal for reference when needing spiritual reinforcement.

- Look for God's hand of favor and protection. This can go unnoticed if our focus is misdirected. But if we discern His helping hand, then we're greatly encouraged.

- At all times and for all things, give thanks in the name of Jesus. Then praise the Lord because He is worthy of honor and glory forever.

For no matter how many promises God has made, they are "Yes" in Christ. And so through him the "Amen" is spoken by us to the glory of God – 2 Corinthians 1:20 NIV.

Dear Lord, our sights are set directly on You—the target of our faith. What a pleasure it is to rest in You and delight in Your perfect love. In all that we do, help us to always glorify You.

_____

_____

_____

_____

_____

_____

_____

_____

_____

_____

_____

_____

_____

Beyond All Comparison

May 3, 2014

Therefore we do not lose heart... For momentary, light affliction is producing for us an eternal weight of glory far beyond all comparison, while we look not at the things which are seen, but at the things which are not seen; for the things which are seen are temporal, but the things which are not seen are eternal – 2 Corinthians 4:16-18 NASB.

Because eternity goes on forever, I'm inspired to make this statement: *Our short lifetime here on Earth—including our pain and suffering—compares to eternity the same as one grain of sand compares to a trillion oceans.* But, since God says these things are "far beyond comparison," my assessment can only fall short. Oceans have boundaries, but eternity does not.

Nevertheless, taking my insufficient metaphor a little farther, we see that our time on Earth will determine the temperature of those "trillion oceans." Their waters could offer the cool blue pleasures of Heaven, or they could boil from the fires of hell. How we spend our life will influence each moment of eternity, not only for us, but for every person in our assigned domain.

Wise choices are essential. We must each decide: Will it be submission to God or devotion to self? Focus on good or attention to evil? Where will I lead the ones I love—to Heaven or to hell?

Our first "wise choice" of total submission to God brings us new life and privileged entrance into His kingdom. After that, our years are filled with much opportunity for spiritual conquest and harvest. But war is never easy. The battles are fierce, and injuries may be severe. Every occasion to fight for good will provoke a counterattack. And why is that? Because so much is at stake—not just for today, but age upon age, forevermore without end.

Unfortunately, the world trains us to strive for affluence and personal achievement as tokens of success. These worldly attainments are most often a sidetrack from doing the will of God. From the Lord's eternal point of view, the persons required to suffer for the sake of His cause are the ones most blessed and honored. The believer who endures needful hardship without resentment is bringing glory to God, in full view of the world.

Then I heard the voice of the Lord, saying, "Whom shall I send, and who will go for Us?" Then I said, "Here am I. Send me!" – Isaiah 6:8 NASB.

Will you answer God's call in the same way that Isaiah did, or will you waste your valuable time with selfish pursuits? Even good pursuits are fruitless if they're not a part of God's plan. For each of us, our tiny grain of time holds exponential power. Today's word or action may expand and echo through the space of eternity, testifying either in Heaven for glory or in Hell for torment and condemnation.

Beginning this very hour, let the Spirit inspire and sanctify your stewardship of time. Kneel before God to repent of any sin—especially judgement and unforgiveness. Don't miss a chance to be patient and kind. Sow the seeds of love and truth in every patch of barren soil. Fight and pray. Loose God's power through many expressions of praise!

Thank You, Lord, for the promise of eternity with You. As we walk in the brief discomforts of this world, please keep the upcoming "weight of glory" always on our minds. Help us face adversity with holiness and power. The tasks ahead are daunting, but we know all things are possible with You.

_____

_____

_____

_____

_____

_____

_____

A Clean Slate

February 23, 2010

Therefore, if anyone is in Christ, he is a new creation; old things have passed away; behold, all things have become new – 2 Corinthians 5:17.

At the time of our salvation, we hear right away that we're a new creation in Christ. We also hear that there is no condemnation for those who abide in Him (Romans 8:1). But decades later, many Christians are not living in the freedom that is theirs. The enemy has methodically beaten them down so they've forgotten the practical reality of being washed clean. Evil spirits have coerced others to treat them badly, so they feel inferior, shameful and powerless. *Does this profile describe you—even just a little?*

Now here is the truth of the matter: Jesus wiped our slates clean and made us new. Therefore, poor treatment from others is never an accurate reflection of who we are. God calls us His beloved. He has made us kings and priests who establish His kingdom here on Earth (Revelation 1:5,6). We can face each day with confidence because God has given us purpose and honor. With the Holy Spirit to guide us, we can respectfully set boundaries for those who've consistently mistreated us. We can walk in peace and joy instead of sadness.

It's important to remember that unkind people are not the real enemy. Satan is the evil fiend behind the scenes, pushing buttons and pulling strings to stir up strife, judgement and reproach—whatever it takes to keep us from reaching our potential in Christ.

Finally, be strong in the Lord and in the strength of his might. Put on the whole armor of God, that you may be able to stand against the schemes of the devil. For we do not wrestle against flesh and blood, but against the rulers, against the authorities, against the cosmic powers over this present darkness, against the spiritual forces of evil in the heavenly places – Ephesians 6:10-12 ESV.

We must ignore those maligning winds that tell us we're not good enough. God's voice is true, and He has declared that we're new and clean and strong in Him. We are destined to overcome evil, and we will do it gloriously when we abide in His love—attended by His amazing grace.

We thank You, Lord, for erasing the sin from our lives. We cherish the freedom to walk through life with our heads held high, no longer bound by shame and condemnation. We rejoice in our royal assignments, and we delight in our priestly concerns.

_____

_____

_____

_____

_____

_____

_____

_____

_____

_____

_____

_____

_____

_____

_____

_____

_____

_____

To God Be the Glory

Thank You, Lord, for the privilege of writing this book.

Thank You for Your perfect love.

Let each reader be thrilled by Your kisses of truth.
Let hearts be transformed to walk uprightly on Your paths of purpose.
Let every cup overflow in the amazing days to come.

All praise and honor and glory are Yours forever!

www.ingramcontent.com/pod-product-compliance
Lightning Source LLC
Chambersburg PA
CBHW060014050426
42448CB00012B/2750